CAMBRIDGE LIBRARY COLLECTION

Books of enduring scholarly value

Travel and Exploration

The history of travel writing dates back to the Bible, Caesar, the Vikings and the Crusaders, and its many themes include war, trade, science and recreation. Explorers from Columbus to Cook charted lands not previously visited by Western travellers, and were followed by merchants, missionaries, and colonists, who wrote accounts of their experiences. The development of steam power in the nineteenth century provided opportunities for increasing numbers of 'ordinary' people to travel further, more economically, and more safely, and resulted in great enthusiasm for travel writing among the reading public. Works included in this series range from first-hand descriptions of previously unrecorded places, to literary accounts of the strange habits of foreigners, to examples of the burgeoning numbers of guidebooks produced to satisfy the needs of a new kind of traveller - the tourist.

The Two Voyages of the *Pandora*

Sir Allen Young (1827–1915), was a merchant navy officer and experienced polar explorer. He took part in several expeditions before those of the *Pandora* including as navigator to McClintock on the *Fox* to discover the fate of Sir John Franklin. He was also in command of the *Fox* on the 1860 North Atlantic Telegraph Expedition to assess the practicality of a cable route between Europe and America across the Faroes, Iceland and Greenland. In 1875 and 1876 he led two expeditions in the Canadian Arctic on the steam yacht *Pandora*. The first, the British North-West Passage Expedition, was an attempt to reach the magnetic pole via Baffin Bay and Lancaster Sound, and to navigate the North-West Passage in one season. The second was a further attempt on the North-West Passage, but also to deliver dispatches to George Nares' Arctic expedition. These compelling accounts were first published together in 1879.

Cambridge University Press has long been a pioneer in the reissuing of out-of-print titles from its own backlist, producing digital reprints of books that are still sought after by scholars and students but could not be reprinted economically using traditional technology. The Cambridge Library Collection extends this activity to a wider range of books which are still of importance to researchers and professionals, either for the source material they contain, or as landmarks in the history of their academic discipline.

Drawing from the world-renowned collections in the Cambridge University Library and other partner libraries, and guided by the advice of experts in each subject area, Cambridge University Press is using state-of-the-art scanning machines in its own Printing House to capture the content of each book selected for inclusion. The files are processed to give a consistently clear, crisp image, and the books finished to the high quality standard for which the Press is recognised around the world. The latest print-on-demand technology ensures that the books will remain available indefinitely, and that orders for single or multiple copies can quickly be supplied.

The Cambridge Library Collection brings back to life books of enduring scholarly value (including out-of-copyright works originally issued by other publishers) across a wide range of disciplines in the humanities and social sciences and in science and technology.

The Two Voyages of the *Pandora*

In 1875 and 1876

ALLEN YOUNG

CAMBRIDGE
UNIVERSITY PRESS

CAMBRIDGE UNIVERSITY PRESS

Cambridge, New York, Melbourne, Madrid, Cape Town,
Singapore, São Paolo, Delhi, Mexico City

Published in the United States of America by Cambridge University Press, New York

www.cambridge.org
Information on this title: www.cambridge.org/9781108050104

© in this compilation Cambridge University Press 2012

This edition first published 1879
This digitally printed version 2012

ISBN 978-1-108-05010-4 Paperback

THE 'PANDORA' BESET AND NIPPED IN MELVILLE BAY, 24TH JULY, 1876.

THE TWO

VOYAGES OF THE 'PANDORA'

IN 1875 AND 1876.

BY

SIR ALLEN YOUNG, R.N.R.,

F.R.G.S., F.R.A.S., Etc.,

COMMANDER OF THE EXPEDITIONS.

LONDON:

EDWARD STANFORD, 55, CHARING CROSS, S.W.

—

1879.

PREFACE.

THIS narrative of the two cruises of the 'Pandora' was intended for private circulation only, but at the suggestion of a few friends I have requested Mr. Stanford to publish it. The volume contains merely a simple record, or log, from notes in my private journal kept on board, and claims no pretensions to literary merit.

A. Y.

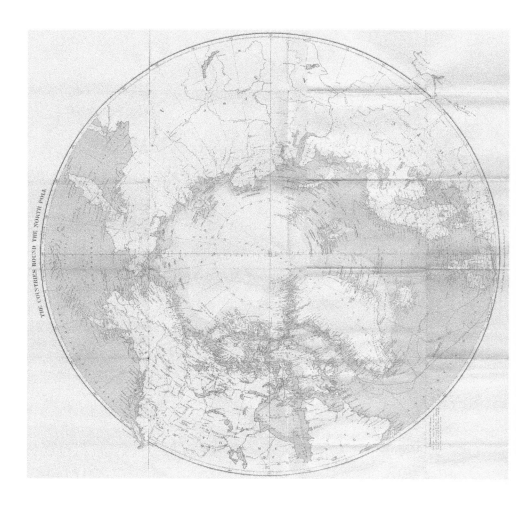

The material originally positioned here is too large for reproduction in this reissue. A PDF can be downloaded from the web address given on page iv of this book, by clicking on 'Resources Available'.

CONTENTS.

I.

THE FIRST VOYAGE OF THE 'PANDORA.'

CHAPTER VII.

CHAPTER VIII.

CHAPTER IX.

CHAPTER X.

CHAPTER XI.

CHAPTER XII.

CHAPTER XIII.

II.

THE SECOND VOYAGE OF THE 'PANDORA.'
1876.

CHAPTER X.

CHAPTER XI.

CHAPTER XII.

CHAPTER XIII.

CHAPTER XIV.

CHAPTER XV.

LIST OF ILLUSTRATIONS.

MAPS.

I.

THE FIRST VOYAGE OF THE 'PANDORA.'

1875.

CHAPTER I.

THE VOYAGE TO GREENLAND.

THE objects of the first voyage of the 'Pandora' in 1875 were to visit the western coast of Greenland, thence to proceed through Baffin's Sea, Lancaster Sound, and Barrow Strait, towards the magnetic pole, and, if practicable, to navigate through the North-West Passage to the Pacific Ocean in one season. As, in following this route, the 'Pandora' would pass King William Island, it was proposed, if successful in reaching that locality, in the summer season, when the snow was off the land, to make a search for further records and for the journals of the ships 'Erebus' and 'Terror.'

As no possible advantage to this project could be gained by wintering, it was arranged that the great loss of time and additional expense attending a ten months' detention in the Arctic Seas should be avoided, if possible, unless such a position could be attained as would render it advisable. In the event, however, of the latter contingency, the 'Pandora' was fully equipped, and the crew were engaged for a period of two years' absence.

The 'Pandora' was built at Devonport, and was first commissioned by Commander W. F. Ruxton, R.N., on the 20th of March, 1863. He sailed in her for the west coast of

B

Africa in the following April, and was posted out of her in December, 1865. Commander E. Stubbs succeeded him, and this was the 'Pandora's' only commission in the Navy, four years on the coast of Africa, returning in 1867. She was built for speed, under sail or steam, or both combined, and fitted with engines of 80-horse power. The 'Pandora' was purchased from the Admiralty, and taken to the works of Messrs. Day and Summers, at Southampton, to be fortified and prepared with all the modern equipments of an Arctic exploring ship. She was rigged as a barquentine, and carried eight boats, including a steam cutter and three whale-boats.

When the repairs and alterations were completed the 'Pandora' was removed to the docks, and provisioned and stored for eighteen months. The officers and crew were selected, and she anchored in the Southampton Water in June to receive her gunpowder, and to make final preparations for her adventurous cruise.

The 'Pandora' carried the white ensign and burgee of the Royal Yacht Squadron, and her complement of officers and men was thirty-one all told, as follows :—

1. ALLEN W. YOUNG,[1] R.N.R.   ..   *Captain.*
2. F. INNES LILLINGSTON,[2] R.N.   .. *Lieutenant.*
3. GEORGE PIRIE,[3] R.N. ..   ..   .. *Lieutenant.*
4. L. B. KOOLEMANS BEYNEN,[4] R.N.N. *Lieutenant.*

---

[1] Sir Allen Young entered the merchant service in 1846. He commanded the 'Marlborough,' East Indiaman, 1500 tons, twice round the world, 1853–54; and the 'Adelaide,' steam troop-ship, 3000 tons, during the Crimean war, 1855–56. He was sailing-master of the 'Fox' (M'Clintock), 1857–59, and commenced his travelling work by laying out a depôt between February 15 and March 3, the thermometer averaging — 40 to — 48; mercury frozen all the time. On his return he started for Fury Beach to get some stores left by Parry, absent from March 18 to 28. He started again on April 7, tracing the south and west shores of Prince of Wales' Land. After thirty-eight days he sent back the men and tent, owing to provisions running short, and went on for forty days with one man and the dogs, sleeping each night in a hole in the snow. He attempted to cross the M'Clintock Channel, and went about forty miles from the land, the ice being frightfully heavy. He reached the ship on June 7, after an absence of seventy-eight days. He went again to explore Peel Sound from June 10 to 28. He then connected Osborn's with Browne's farthest, and discovered 380 miles of new coast line. He

5.	A. C. Horner	..	..	..	..	*Surgeon and Naturalist.*
6.	Mr. De Wilde	..	..	..	..	*Artist.*
7.	J. A. MacGahan	..	..	..	..	*Correspondent.*
8.	Benjamin Ball	..	..	..	..	*First Engineer.*
9.	Archibald Porteous	..	..	..	..	*Second Engineer.*
10.	Harry Toms [5]	..	..	..	..	*Gunner.*
11.	Robert James	..	..	..	..	*Carpenter.*
12.	Henry Mitchell	..	..	..	..	*Boatswain.*
13.	John Mott	..	..	..	..	*Sailmaker.*
14.	William Edwards	..	..	..	..	*Ship's Steward.*
15.	Joseph Lawrence	..	..	..	..	*Ward-room Steward.*
16.	Thomas Florance [6]	..	..	..	..	*Captain of Hold.*
17.	Joseph Shelton	..	..	..	..	*Cook.*
18.	Eskimo Joe	..	..	..	..	*Interpreter.*
19.	Henry Andrews	..	..	..	..	*Quartermaster.*
20.	William Randerson	..	..	..	..	*Quartermaster.*
21.	James Timpson	..	..	..	..	*Quartermaster.*
22.	Henry Mihill	..	..	..	..	*Quartermaster.*
23.	Charles Vine	..	..	..	..	*Captain's Coxswain.*
24.	Charles Tizzard	..	..	.	..	*Boatswain's Mate.*
25.	Allan Gillies	..	..	..	..	*Harpooneer.*
26.	Edward Grace	..	..	..	..	*Able Seaman.*
27.	William Davis	..	..	..	..	*Able Seaman.*
28.	James Pennington	..	..	..	..	*Able Seaman.*
29.	G. W. Thorne	..	..	..	..	*Able Seaman.*
30.	Edwin Griffey	..	..	..	..	*Blacksmith and Stoker.*
31.	James Cole	..	..	..	..	*Stoker.*

---

became a Lieutenant of the Naval Reserve, February 24, 1862. F.R.G.S. and F.R.A.S. He commanded the 'Fox' in the North Atlantic Telegraph Expedition in 1862, going to Faroe Isles, Iceland, and Greenland; and the 'Quantung' in the European Chinese Navy, 1862–64. He was Commissioner to the Maritime Congress at Naples in 1871. (See 'Arctic Navy List.')

Sir Allen is author of an account of the voyage of the 'Fox,' in the first number of the 'Cornhill Magazine'; republished in 1875 by Mr. Griffin, of Portsea.

[2] Lieutenant in the Royal Navy, on the retired list, September 7, 1871.

[3] Navigating Sub-Lieutenant in the Royal Navy, on the active list, July 27, 1870. He was promoted to the rank of Lieutenant on October 13, 1876, and is now serving on board H.M.S. 'Nassau,' surveying ship.

[4] Lieutenant in the Royal Dutch Navy, and had served in the Sumatra Squadron, and on shore in the naval brigade at Achin.

[5] Mr. Toms was a Quartermaster in the 'Fox,' with Sir Leopold M'Clintock, during her memorable voyage in 1857–59.

[6] Thomas Florance served in the 'North Star,' under Captain Pullen, 1852–54, and also in the 'Fox,' with Sir Leopold M'Clintock, as stoker.

The expenses of the expedition, and the purchase and equipment of the 'Pandora,' were undertaken by myself; and I was assisted by contributions from the late Lady Franklin, who never ceased to take the greatest interest in Arctic matters ; from Mr. James Gordon Bennett, who was desirous of sending a correspondent; and from Lieutenant Lillingston, who accompanied me as second in command.

On the 25th of June, everything being reported ready for sea, we slipped from the buoy off the Southampton Pier, and proceeded round to Portsmouth. We had already received on board two bags of letters for the 'Alert' and 'Discovery,' besides parcels, which had been forwarded in the hope of our being able to deliver them, or deposit them at the entrance of Smith Sound. On entering Portsmouth harbour, a message was received from the Admiral to the effect that we might go alongside the dockyard, and we accordingly moored by the Queen's Steps at 9 P.M. I was much touched by the hearty sympathy which I received at Portsmouth. I had endeavoured, from the commencement, to keep our cruise quite unnoticed, and had carefully avoided all demonstrations; but, as we passed out of Portsmouth harbour, the crews of all Her Majesty's ships gave us hearty cheers, to which we responded in the best manner we could with our little crew, and by dipping our colours.

We arrived at Cowes in the evening of the 26th of June, where I had to meet Mr. Harper, our agent, who came to examine the accounts with me, and to make final arrangements for the pay of the crew, and for the payment of allotments to their wives and families.

Having taken farewell of my friends at Cowes, I embarked at midnight, intending to sail for Plymouth on the first of the ebb next morning. Accordingly, on the 27th we slipped from the buoy at 4 A.M. It was a lovely morning, with scarcely a breath of wind, as we passed out through the Needles, and proceeded with all fore-and-aft canvas. As we passed Portland, H.M.S. 'Warrior' signalled, "Wish you all success;" and, in answer, we signalled our thanks. Passing close round the Bill, we caught a fair wind from the southward, and made all sail, letting the steam run down. I was pleased with the performance of the ship under canvas; she made a good six knots with the screw down.

Arriving at Plymouth at 9 A.M., I immediately sent on shore for ten tons of coal, and also asked Lieut. Lillingston to call upon Admiral Sir H. Keppel, and to express my regret that I was unable to come personally. By the time we had completed our coaling, Admiral Keppel and Earl Mount Edgecumbe most kindly came on board to greet us, and to say good-bye. At six o'clock we steamed out. When off the Eddystone we made all plain sail and stopped the engines, steering off to S.W. with a light N.W. breeze, and, having set the watch, we all turned in. At noon, on the 29th, we passed the Lizard, and at 1.20 sent letters on board the ship 'Queen of Australia,' from Calcutta, bound for Dundee.

After the 18th of July, we experienced nothing but alternate west winds and calms, with generally a high swell from the westward. We continued beating to windward, taking advantage of everything in our favour; but we made but slow progress, owing to our being laden so deep. On the 19th, we were in lat. 58° 58' N., long. 31° 33' W. I had endeavoured to get to the northward, in hopes of some change in the weather, which seemed so unusual for this season, and so opposite to our experience when crossing in the 'Fox.

We constantly saw finner whales (*Physalus antiquorum*[1]) generally going to the northward. Since the 12th, we had

---

[1] *Balænoptera antiquorum* of Gray is the big finner, rorqual, or razor back, a cetacean from 60 to 70 feet long, black above and white below, with the flippers black. The old name given by Fabricius is *Balæna physalus*. The Eskimo name is *Tunnolik*. It is not seen farther north than Rifkol.

been accompanied by mallemokes (*Fulmar petrels*[1]), and since the 16th by a number of shearwaters (*Puffinus anglorum*[2]), which we passed in flocks on the water. We had calms on the 23rd, 24th, and 25th, with light winds from N. and N.E., followed by a fresh N.W. to W. wind on the 26th, when we were in lat. 57° 55′, long. 42° 49′, Cape Farewell being N. 17, W. 119 miles. On the 27th, boarded the 'Traveller,' of Peterhead, and obtained newspapers, and proceeded in company with her on the 28th, on which day we saw the first icebergs. The next morning we had a fresh breeze from the E.S.E., and at five saw the first Spitzbergen ice. We passed a few straggling pieces, and at 6 P.M. came upon several streams of ice. I then kept away to the westward, but finding that the wind was increasing, and a thick fog coming on to seaward, I steered in to the N.E. to go through the ice, and to get into the land water. At noon, we were in lat. 60° 14′ N., long. 68° 20′ W., the land about Cape Desolation being plainly in sight whenever it cleared. Throughout the afternoon we were sailing through heavy ice, and received some severe blows; but towards evening, as we hauled into the land, the wind decreased to a calm and light N.E. air, and the ice was very close. On many of the heavy pieces we saw the bladder-nosed seals (*Cystophora cristata*[3]) lying basking, and, as we ranged the ship up near them, several fell victims to our sportsmen. These seals are quite unused to seeing human beings, for they appeared to take no notice of the ship beyond

---

[1] The *Mallemoke*, or "foolish fly" of Crantz (i. p. 86), is the "Molly" of the whalers, the birds which come in greedy crowds to feed on the carcases of the whales. It is the *Procellaria glacialis*, or Fulmar petrel, called *Kakordluk* by the Eskimos, and the black variety *Igarsok*.

[2] The Manx shearwater (*Puffinus anglorum*) is not an Arctic bird, and is not met with north of the entrance of Davis Strait.

[3] The bladder-nose seal (*Cystophora cristata*) is one of the largest in Greenland. Its name is due to a curious bladder-like appendage on its forehead connected with the nostrils, which can be blown up at will. The Danish name is *klapmyd*, the Eskimo *neitersoak* and *nesausolik*.

raising their heads, and had we been in pursuit of them, we might have killed any number. I am surprised that some enterprising fisherman does not send out a ship or small vessel properly equipped for seal-hunting. A number of boats sent away from such a vessel amongst the ice in fine weather might secure a rich harvest of skins and oil.

In the evening of the 29th, being almost surrounded by heavy ice, and anxious to get into the land water, I got up steam for the first time since leaving England. We proceeded until 9 P.M., when we made fast to a floe to pick up some seals that were shot in passing, and to get fresh water, of which we had been sadly in want, owing to our long passage. We found this water deliciously soft and pure upon the surface of the floe-piece, and we remained until 11 P.M., when we cast off, and steamed slowly on towards the land. It was a brilliant night, almost calm, and with a clear sky, and as we approached the land the ice became slacker. By 4 A.M., on the 30th, we got into the land water at about fifteen miles distant from the shore. We passed many seals lying on the ice-floes, and numbers of birds in flocks were on the ice, in the water, and flying around us.

CHAPTER II.

THE CRYOLITE MINE.

WE were now off the entrance to Arsuk Fiord,[1] the high land of Sermilik[2] bearing N.E.,[3] and we could, after a short study of the coast, distinguish Storö, and the two cones of Umanak.[4] The whole coast from S.E. to N.N.E. stood before us like a panorama, and the sea was so calm, and everything so still and peaceful, excepting now and then the rumbling of an overturning berg, or the distant echo of the floes as they pressed together to seaward of us, that it almost seemed like a transition to some other world. It was indeed enchantment, after the constant rolling of the ocean, and the crashing amongst the outside ice, which we had experienced during the previous afternoon. I now determined to proceed to Ivigtut to endeavour to get twenty tons of coal, and to steam to Disco in the event of the weather being calm; we therefore turned the 'Pandora's' bow towards Storö, and soon approached the land. We found our late companion, the 'Traveller,' becalmed under the land, and surrounded with loose ice, so I went alongside, and offered to tow her into Ivigtut, a distance of sixteen miles. Of this offer the Captain gladly availed himself, as he did not otherwise expect to get in for at least two days, there being always a strong surface current running out of

---

[1] This coast is the *West Bygd* of the ancient Norse colonizers of Greenland. Near Arsuk was the old Norse church of Steinnaes.

[2] *Sermilik* means "having a glacier," from *sermek*, "ice formed on the land."

[3] All the bearings are true, unless stated to be magnetic.

[4] The word *Umanak*, from *umit* "the heart," is frequently used as a name for conical-shaped islands. This *Umanak* is the Cape Comfort of our old Elizabethan navigators.

the fiords at this season, caused by the mountain rivers, and the melting of the last remnants of the snow.

When inside the fiord, the wind sprung up and freshened from the S.E., which somewhat delayed us, and we did not arrive off Ivigtut until 4 P.M., when, finding that I could be supplied with coal, and not wishing to let go my anchor in thirty fathoms, according to the custom here, I went alongside the barque 'Thor' by the permission of her captain. She was lying alongside a jetty, or rather stage, rigged out from the shore, and was being loaded with cryolite; as she was securely moored, we were enabled to wheel the coal across in barrows. We found Mr. Fritz, the Manager of the Cryolite Company, most obliging and courteous. He offered us every assistance, and any supplies that we might require, besides pressing us to accept his private stock of pigs, which I declined; but he insisted on sending me one small pig for the ship's company, and a large hamper of the most delicious radishes, which he had grown in the open air. Nothing could exceed his kindness, and I wish here to record it, and to mention that anyone going to Ivigtut is certain of a hearty welcome and the utmost attention from Mr. Fritz.

We found the 'Fox,' my old ship, lying there, looking quite smart, and evidently kept in good repair. I went on board with Toms to have a look at the old craft which had been our home for two-and-a-half years, and I felt an inclination to linger there, and even some desire to exchange for the 'Pandora,' although as yet the 'Pandora' has behaved in all respects to my satisfaction.

Immediately we were secured I gave leave to all hands, and notwithstanding the myriads of mosquitoes, which rendered the shore intolerable, all the men went on excursions, their principal desire being apparently to exchange articles of European manufacture for anything of native workmanship, much to the advantage of the natives. They also searched for a cat, as we had left without one, to which circumstance all our head winds were attributed. The result of their search was that we secured at least three cats and a pig. The mallemoke " Billy," which was caught off Farewell, and shorn of its wing, is kept as a pet on board.

Ivigtut is situated about sixteen miles up the fiord named Arsuk, after the lofty island of that name, which borders the left, or rather the northern side of the fiord, and is composed of granite, with overlying syenite. The granite continues for about eight miles up the fiord on both sides, when it disappears, and alternates with gneiss. This gneiss forms the shore on both sides of the fiord for from seven to eight miles up to the spot named Ivigtut by the natives, where the cryolite[1] is found. The name Ivigtut was given to this place by the natives on account of its fertility. *Ivik* means grass, and *Ivigtut* is the plural of *Ivigtok*, "rich in grass." Ivigtut was first frequented by the Eskimos for the purpose of fishing and drying the Arctic salmon, but was deserted on account of the increasing floating ice. We owe the discovery of cryolite to a peculiar circumstance. The Greenlanders employed the water-worn fragments of this mineral as weights for their fishing lines, and in this shape the first specimens were sent by the missionaries to Copenhagen as ethnographical curiosities. The cryolite is found near the shore, resting immediately upon the gneiss. The purest is of a snow-white colour, without any intermixture of foreign substances. The grayish-white variety which lies on the surface is considered the second quality of commerce. It very much resembles ice which has been curved and grooved by the action of the sun's rays. In 1857 a license was given to a private company for working the cryolite. The number of men employed generally, amounts to one hundred

---

[1] Cryolite is a very rare mineral, found only in the gneiss of West Greenland. It is the double hydrofluate of soda and alumina. The name is from κρυος, hoar frost, and λιθος, stone. It melts like ice in the flame of a candle, hence the name.

in summer, and thirty in winter, besides the superintendent and other officers. The workmen are relieved at fixed periods. They do not bring any of their families with them, and generally contract to remain three years, the mines being worked both winter and summer; a smaller mine, more free from snow, being usually worked throughout the autumnal and winter months. From 1857 to 1866 the number of tons exported was 14,000, in eighty ship-loads; and from 1867 to 1875 the quantity was 70,000 tons, being an average of twenty-six ship-loads each year. The cryolite is used for a variety of purposes, but principally for making soda, and also in the United States for preparing aluminium.[1]

At the time of our visit, the ships 'Thor' of Hamburg, and the 'Alibi' of Peterhead, were both loading a cargo, and the 'Traveller,' of the latter place, which we had just towed in, was regularly employed in carrying cryolite to Copenhagen. The 'Fox,' so celebrated in Arctic history, is now in the employ of the Company, and is used for bringing out supplies and reliefs of workmen to the colony. The cryolite is all brought from the mine (which is, perhaps, 200 yards from the sea) to the beach close to the shipping stage, and is stacked in large, square heaps, as being the most convenient for measuring it both for shipment and for the royalty to be paid to the Royal Danish Greenland Company.

I was so occupied on board that I had no time to make more than a very short visit to the mine. I then walked up the rising ground, being attracted by a large wooden cross marking the burying ground of the little colony. It was a well-chosen spot, where vegetation flourished, and away from the works and habitations, commanding a lovely view of the fiord

[1] For accounts of the cryolite mine, see a paper of Sir Charles Geisecké, in the 'Edinburgh Philosophical Journal,' vi. p. 141; and a paper by J. W. Tayler, Esq., in the 'Quarterly Journal' of the Geological Society,' xii. p. 140. These papers have been reprinted in the 'Arctic Manual,' pp. 341 and 344. See also 'Danish Greenland, its People and its Products,' by Dr. Henry Rink, pp. 79 and 313.

and surrounding mountains.   The cross bore the beautiful and
appropriate inscription taken from Psalm cxxxix. 7–10 :

"Whither shall I go from Thy Spirit? or whither
Shall I fly from Thy presence?
If I ascend up into heaven, Thou art there: if I
Make my bed in hell, behold, Thou art there.
If I take the wings of the morning, and dwell in the uttermost parts of the sea;
Even there shall Thy hand lead me, and Thy right hand shall hold me."

It was with a deep feeling of sadness that I noticed several
smaller crosses, marking the last resting-place of the poor
colonists who had left their native country to die in this
desolate place; and, with an earnest reflection on the above
sacred words, I returned on board the ship to obtain a few
hours' rest previous to sailing on the following morning.

CHAPTER III.

NAVIGATION ON THE COAST OF GREENLAND.

HAVING received twenty-eight tons of coal, I started at 3 A.M. and steamed slowly out of the fiord. A fog which set in soon afterwards made me very anxious, as the water is too deep to anchor. I had no pilot, and had never been here before, and at one moment I thought of returning to the anchorage at Ivigtut, as the only place I could make, but fortunately, on rounding the western extremity of the island of Arsuk, the fog partially cleared, and we found a fresh S.E. wind blowing out of the fiord, to which we immediately made sail, and passed out to sea without further difficulty. We soon fell in with streams of ice, which were apparently being driven along the coast from the south, and out of the great bays about Juliane-haab.[1] The wind also increased, and we ran at some speed under reefed topsails to the northward, avoiding the ice as much as possible, but sometimes receiving a smart blow. Our artist took some hydrographic sketches of the coast, and of the entrance to Arsuk Fiord, which if published will be of some service to future navigators of this fiord, the entrance of which is becoming of some importance, and is most difficult to make from the sea without a knowledge of the appearance of the land. We continued running with a fair wind all the afternoon, though the ice compelled us to deviate greatly from a straight course, and by night it came on thick with rain, and so dark that the floes and floe-pieces could only be avoided

[1] The southernmost Danish Greenland colony (in 60° 43′ N.), but not the southern-most settlement. Farther south there are the Moravian missions of Lichtenau and Frederiksdal, close to Cape Farewell.

with great difficulty. I was up all night, and hoped for better weather next morning, but the wind now increased to a fresh gale from the southward, and the ice became very close in some of the streams. We continued running through streams along the coast, as to seaward the pack seemed much closer. At 7 A.M. on the morning of the 1st of August I close-reefed, in the event of our having to round-to, but we succeeded in getting into clear water about noon. The barometer had fallen considerably, and I fully expected a heavy gale, especially as the rain began to come down in torrents, and the weather to thicken. In the forenoon we had to haul out of a heavy jam of ice pressed upon a long reef of islands and rocks which extended above our bows, among which the larger pieces had grounded, and had brought up the floe, forming a lee shore of the wildest description. Having cleared the western extremity of this danger, we again bore away, and at noon passed close to the " Vaidoe Island," just off the entrance to the colony of Frederikshaab. But the thick weather prevented our seeing more than the outlying isles and rocks, which we passed at one mile distant.

In the afternoon we again passed through a very heavy stream of ice, and on approaching the outer edge I heard the sea breaking violently amongst the floes. I took this as an indication that we were getting clear, and to the northern limit of the Spitzbergen drift ice. Shortly afterwards, in getting into more water, we suddenly experienced a heavy swell, and I then knew that we need not expect much more of this troublesome and dangerous enemy. In the evening we were approaching the glacier which extends down to the sea north of the Tallart Bank, and about twenty-eight miles north of Frederikshaab. It is the most conspicuous mark upon the coast of Greenland, and cannot be mistaken. Our artist took a view of it. I remember that when we pushed through the Spitzbergen ice in the 'Fox,' the first landfall we made was this glacier, which immediately directed us to the position of Frederikshaab. In sailing through ice, especially if very close, it is difficult to keep the reckoning, and as such navigation is also often accompanied by thick weather, it is necessary, if possible, to have a sure landmark.

The night proved better than I expected. The wind moderated, but the rain continued in torrents, and we passed through a quantity of drift masses of ice, which I supposed had been hung up by bergs grounded off the Tallart Bank and the glacier. But it was too dark to see anything, and we continued through the gloom with a good look-out, the ship rolling with her heavy deck-load, and everything dripping with rain and fog.

The morning of the 2nd of August broke thick with rain, but to my great relief no ice was passed. The wind fell off to nearly a calm, and as I fancied we must be near or over the southernmost Torske Bank,[1] I sounded, and found twenty-five fathoms. We immediately stopped, and put over some fishing lines, but without success, as a light wind, with a current to the north, prevented us from keeping our lines on the bottom. The only things brought up were some conglomerate composed of ascidiæ inside horny cases, and outside the cases bivalve molluscs, and several common log worms.

We steamed to the northward, and during the afternoon I observed many terns,[2] kittiwakes,[3] and a few looms.[4] The surface of the water was frequently rippled as if by a strong current; many pieces of drift ice were also passed, from all which I hoped we were setting to the northward. We passed one large iceberg, apparently aground, about 2 P.M. Its

---

[1] *Torske* is Danish for a cod-fish.

[2] The Arctic tern (*Sterna Arctica*, or *Sterna macroura*) is a beautiful little sea-swallow with red legs and beak. The Eskimo name is *Imerkoteilak*.

[3] The kittiwake is a graceful Arctic gull (*Rissa tridactyla*, or *Larus tridactylus* of Fabricius). The Eskimo name is *Taterak*.

[4] Brunnick's guillemot (*Alca arra*, or *Uria arra*); in Eskimo, *Agpa*.

summit was crowded with birds, which from the distance appeared to be terns, apparently waiting for the fog to clear off to resume their flight. The mist disappearing, we had a lovely night; but the wind continuing light from the N.W., we kept slowly steaming to the N.N.E.

We had been eating some of the seal beef, which we procured in passing through the ice, and it was generally appreciated by the officers, and especially by "Joe," but at present the crew, as might be expected, rather looked with disdain upon it, and did not seem to care for it. They soon found out its value, as it is certainly the most nutritious and wholesome food in this part of the world, and by steeping it well and boiling it twice over it is, in my opinion, equal to very tender ox beef.

We continued to the northward under steam during the 3rd, the wind still blowing directly against us. At eleven o'clock we saw the islands outside Ny Sukkertoppen,[1] and could make out through the fog the high conical mount which stands out from the mainland, and so well marks the approach to the colony. At noon the wind changed to the south. So we ceased steaming, and passed within a mile of the islands off Ny Sukkertoppen, on the largest of which we noticed a white wooden beacon, or staff, with cross pieces at the top. The current ran north, and caused strong ripples on the surface. We now also noticed flights of eider drakes for the first time—they were going seaward, and came in constant flocks from the land.

During the whole of the 4th of August we had a light north wind, with clear sky, mild weather, and a hot sun. I stood in towards the land, coasting about a mile off, until off the entrance to Surk-ström Fiord at noon, when we suddenly found ourselves among a labyrinth of reefs and rocks not marked in the chart, which I named Pandora Reefs, and on

---

[1] "Ny," or New Sukkertoppen (sugar-loaf), is south of the older settlement of Sukkertoppen, which was founded in 1755, in 65° 20' N.

one of which we touched slightly. I then hauled out to W.N.W., the wind being still northward, and cleared all the dangers. The splendid scenery stood like a panorama before us, and as we passed Surk-ström Fiord our artist made a sketch of this beautiful arm of the sea, which penetrates direct inland thirty or forty miles, having precipitous mountains on each side 4000 to 5000 feet high, and reaching to the inland ice, which we could plainly see at the head. I then thought of standing off to the Torske Bank to catch some cod-fish, and was proceeding N.N.W., under very easy steam and fore-and-aft canvas, when on stopping to sound we observed some natives coming off in their kayaks. They had had a long pull, as we were now at least sixteen miles from the land; and although we had been standing off at five miles an hour, they had never given up the chase, and now overtook us. They brought salmon, fresh and smoked, and a few eggs, and all that the poor fellows asked in exchange for eighteen of these fine fish, was a few biscuits and a little tobacco. They had pulled so hard that they were quite wet through with the sea, so we hoisted them all in, gave them a good warming in the engine-room, and a glass of grog, and they took their leave quite happy and contented. They belonged to Old Sukkertoppen, but were staying for the present at a place called Kangek,[1] just north of Surkström Fiord, catching salmon and reindeer.

I had limited the engineers to 3 cwt. of coal per hour, and we could not therefore steam more than four knots. The wind was west, alternating with calms, until 4 A.M., when a breeze sprung up from the southward, and we set all canvas, and at 8 A.M. stopped the engines. We passed the Knight Islands, off the colony of Holsteinborg,[2] on the 5th, and at

---

[1] Kangek means a cape or headland. The name frequently occurs along the coast of Greenland.

[2] At this time H.M.S. 'Valorous' was in Holsteinborg harbour undergoing repairs, after having run upon a reef of rocks not marked on the chart, on July 27. The 'Valorous' left Holsteinborg on August 8.

noon were in lat. 67° 11′ N., long. 54° 26′ W., steering along the land, our artist being busy all day making hydrographic sketches of the coast at the most interesting points. At 6 P.M. we sounded in eighteen fathoms, and found shells, sand, and particles of granite.

I was on deck during the whole night, as we were passing close to Rifkol, the water being very shallow, and the islands very low. In the morning we had passed Rifkol, and had gone inside the rocks laid down in the chart. The coast here was quite changed in appearance, and the transition from the high snow-capped mountains to a low, irregular tract, quite devoid of snow, was very remarkable. I had intended, on the previous evening, to stop at the Rifkol Bank to try to catch some hallibut and cod, and we sounded in seventeen fathoms, finding sand, shells, and small stones from the granite rocks; but a light breeze sprang up, and being so anxious to get onward, I gave up the attempt.

CHAPTER IV.

GODHAVN AND THE WAIGAT.

THE island of Disco had been in sight since seven in the morning of the 6th of August, at a distance of nearly seventy miles. We continued to the N.N.E., passing to windward of the Whalefish Islands and the solitary islet west of the Hunde Islands, upon which we observed thousands of birds, apparently roosting.

The bay of Disco, and the grand cliffs and snow-covered table-land of the island to the northward, were now spread out before us, and to the eastward were Jacobshavn and Christianshaab. Numbers of whales of the finned species were blowing in all directions, and the sea was everywhere dotted with icebergs, the whole forming, in the clear, bright atmosphere, a most enchanting scene. We passed close to windward of the Whalefish Islands, and the two flat islets south of Godhavn, upon one of which we so nearly ran the 'Fox' in a gale and snow storm in May, 1858.[1] On approaching the high land, the wind fell lighter and more baffling, and, with our slow steaming, it was not till midnight that we arrived off the entrance to Lievely.

On the 7th of August I observed a whale-boat approaching, and received on board Mr. Elborg, the Governor, who had kindly come out to meet us, bringing me letters from Captain Nares and Mr. Clements Markham. I learned that the 'Alert' and 'Discovery' had arrived at Disco on the 6th of July, after a very severe passage across the Atlantic and in Davis Strait. They had, after staying nine days in harbour, transhipped

---

[1] See M'Clintock's 'Fate of Franklin,' p. 118.

stores from the 'Valorous,' and proceeded northward on the 15th, intending to stop at Ritenbenk and Upernivik, to ship more dogs. The 'Valorous' had left Godhavn at the same time, having proceeded to the coal mine in the Waigat, and intending thence to go southward to make observations in sounding and dredging in Davis Strait. I consequently addressed all letters for that ship to the Secretary of the Admiralty, as there was now no chance of our meeting her. We anchored in Godhavn, but found no other ship there, the Company's vessel having left for home the previous evening; but, as another was expected in about a fortnight, we wrote up our letters, and having filled up some water and given the crew general leave and a dance on shore, we departed at midnight for the Waigat. There I expected to find coal already dug out for us by the natives under the direction of Mr. Krarup Smith, the Inspector of North Greenland, who had kindly undertaken this work for me at the request of Mr. Clements Markham.

On the 8th of August we were steaming slowly along the south shore of Disco, in charmingly mild weather, which rendered a change of clothing necessary. Thousands of icebergs were around us.

The fisheries of Disco appear to be falling off more and more every year, and recently but few whales have been taken. The seals, moreover, are much scarcer than formerly. I noticed no seal meat or fresh skins, and, in fact, the natives appear to be quite at a standstill, except the few who were away at the large fiord at the west side of the island, catching salmon. Perhaps this apparent idleness may have been the result of their having received a good sum of money during the long stay of the three Government ships.

We steamed leisurely along towards the coaling cliffs, which is on the Disco shore, about thirty miles inside the Waigat. As we opened the straits, a strong north wind blew against us, bringing up so dense a fog that it was with the greatest difficulty we could clear the numerous icebergs. The season seemed an exceptional one, as from former experience I did not expect to meet with anything like the number of bergs which almost choked up the straits, rendering the navigation very intricate. At midnight we were beset by very thick weather, not being able to see much beyond the jib-boom, and, the water being too deep to hold out any hope of anchoring, we were compelled to proceed, under steam, at a very slow rate, until I decided to moor to a promising looking piece, which we went nearly stem on to. It was a berg which had turned over, and was consequently very smooth and slippery. After several attempts it was secured with two large ice-anchors, and I hoped to be able to ride by it until the gale decreased or the fog cleared. We sounded in fifty-eight fathoms, and supposed we were about a mile from the Disco shore (the mountain on the point at the entrance to the Waigat bearing west), and that the berg was aground; but it afterwards floated with the flood tide and turned over, and began drifting with us upon a group of other bergs.

I was disturbed at three in the morning of the 9th by the noise of the falling over of the berg, and the officer of the watch rushing down to tell me that it had capsized, taking our anchors a long way under water. I still held on until the rolling of the berg released the anchors, when we were once more compelled to steam off into the fog. During the forenoon the sun appeared and the wind decreased, enabling us to obtain the latitude by means of one of Captain George's artificial horizons on deck. We found that we were a little to the northward of Ujaragsugssuk,[1] the point at which I wished

---

[1] From *Ujarak*, which means a stone. The suffix, *Sugssuk*, is only known in names of places. Ujaragsugssuk consists of two wooden houses and about twenty Eskimo huts. It is about twenty miles from the coal mine of Kudliset, on the Disco side, close to the shore, on an abrupt rocky point. It may be found by the bay between Atanekerdluk and Sakak, on the Nugsuak peninsula, being exactly open. On Isunguak Point there are two peaks, the northern very sharp and remarkable, resembling a cairn, and a good mark for finding Ujaragsugssuk, as it is four miles from Isunguak Point. Narsak was not seen in passing, and there appears to be no habitation between Ujaragsugssuk and Kuldiset.

*

to communicate with the natives, and to present a letter to the
Factor with reference to the coaling of the ship. Ujaragsugssuk is not marked on the chart. It lies on the Disco shore,
about half-way between the entrance to the straits and the coal
deposits at Kudliset. After a little delay we saw two houses,
but all our efforts with the steam whistle failed to produce any
effect upon the occupants, who were probably taking a good
forenoon's sleep, being compelled by the dense fog to remain
inactive. On a closer approach, however, the good people of
Ujaragsugssuk were aroused by the whistle; dogs, men, and
women were rushing about, and we were soon boarded by a
kayaker, who informed me that Mr. Jansen, the Governor,
would be on shore to receive me. So I landed, and found
that we were on an outlying station of the Ritenbenk district,
containing about a hundred people, presided over by Governor
Jansen. On landing, a letter from Mr. Clements Markham
was handed to me. It stated that the 'Valorous'[1] had lately
been at the Kudliset mines, and had in five days taken in
105 tons. Markham also informed me that the coals were
cleared for us, and the Governor said that I should meet a
sloop which was coming from the mines, and that I might take
from her sixteen men and five women to assist in loading the
'Pandora.' At Ujaragsugssuk there were a great number of
splendid dogs, of which I purchased four, giving six rixdollars
for each, that price including the harness, and some shark's
flesh for food.

Proceeding to Kudliset, we met the sloop, took in the men
and women, and arrived at the mines at 7 P.M., anchoring in
seven fathoms, and about a quarter of a mile from the beach.
We then gave the Eskimos a good supper all round and turned
in, the men sleeping in the squaresail on deck, and the women,

---

[1] The 'Valorous' was at anchor off the *Kulbrud*, or coal mine of Kudliset, in the
Waigat, from the 17th to the 21st of July. In eighty-eight hours the men got on board
105 tons of coal.

three of whom were remarkably pretty girls, being stowed away in the chart-room, under the guardianship of an old lady, who was evidently the strictest of chaperons, and would not allow one of them to be out of her sight for a moment.

The morning of the 10th was very clear and calm. All hands were sent on shore at 5 A.M., and by dint of real good work we succeeded in getting on board about forty tons[1] by 7 P.M. We then got ready for sea, intending to start as soon as the crew had taken a few hours' rest, they being much fatigued with the day's work. I found the steam cutter of the greatest assistance in towing the boats to and from our ship. At nine we were aroused by a berg coming athwart hawse, but by veering cable we succeeded in clearing our bows of it. I then settled with the Eskimos who had helped us, and having packed up my letters for England, I sent all the natives away to an empty house about a mile distant.

[1] The coal lies imbedded in sandstone underlying the trap formation and close down to the sea-level, in seams of from one to seven feet in thickness. The coal is easily excavated and thrown on the beach, and thence taken to the boats. In the spring, when the ice foot exists, it forms a natural wharf, and a ship or lighter might go almost alongside and take the coal direct on board. An analysis of this coal was made by Professor Fyte, of King's College, Aberdeen, as follows :

Specific Gravity, 1·3848.

Volatile matter	50·6
Coke, consisting of ash	9·84
Carbon	39·56
	100·00

*

CHAPTER V.

THE PASSAGE THROUGH MELVILLE BAY.

RISING at four o'clock on the 11th, I took a last look at the scene. It reminded me forcibly of my former visit in the 'Fox,' which seemed but yesterday, even to the mountain stream which still poured over the summit of the highest ridge, falling in a perpendicular silver line for many hundreds of feet. We were a week later this time, and the season was getting on so fast, that it was with a feeling of relief that I ordered the anchor to be weighed. I felt satisfied with the success of our cruise thus far, and did not anticipate another detention.[1] By the afternoon we had sailed and steamed as far as Hare Island, when the wind suddenly shifted to the northward, and we furled all sails, and continued throughout the night with very easy steam, making slow progress. On the 12th we were under Svarte-Huk, and made a tack off from within a quarter of a mile of the beach, experiencing a strong northward set as we rounded this extraordinary cape. In the evening we could see Sanderson's Hope, and passed close outside the islands, in fine weather and with light north winds.

The morning of the 13th of August was ushered in with

---

[1] Our latitude was 70° 4' 54" N., and longitude 52° 59' 30" W., var. 69° 4', on the 10th of August. This places the coast on the Disco Island side of the Waigat farther to the N.E., and altogether different from the Admiralty charts. The coal mine may easily be found if the opposite coast is in sight, even when Disco is enveloped in fog, by observing a very sharp needle peak called Manik, which bears N. 52° E. from the mine. Behind the mine two mountains rise to about 3000 feet, with a remarkable stream of water flowing over the highest ridge. The 'Valorous' made the latitude of a position at the coal cliff near where her men were working 70° 3' 24" N.

light south winds, and I decided to stop off Upernivik to send my last letters home, so we steered in between the two eastern-most of the Woman's Islands, and entered Upernivik Bay, rounding to close off the settlement.[1] The Governor came on board, and informed us that the 'Alert' and 'Discovery' had left on the 22nd July, and that he considered it to be a very favourable season for them, although on the day they sailed there was a good deal of ice outside the Woman's Islands and to the northward, which obliged them to steer out west.

Having sent a present to the wife of the Governor, and purchased a few sealskin clothes and two more dogs, we bore away, the weather threatening from the S.W. and a heavy rain falling, and passed out between the Talbot Reef and the nearest islands, steering away to N.N.W., and con-tinuing through the night under canvas.

At 7 A.M. on the 14th we could just distinguish the Horse Head, and flocks of looms continually crossed, flying to the westward, from which I inferred that the middle ice was not far out in that direction. We saw numbers of single birds, and hen birds with single young ones, feeding in the water; but the flight of the strong birds was seaward, without resting near the ship. In the afternoon we passed through a long chain of huge icebergs, lying north and south as far as the eye could reach, and, the weather clearing off, we found ourselves close to the outermost of the Duck Islands. We got good

---

[1] In approaching Upernivik two rocks were observed just above water, Sanderson's Hope bearing about E.S.E. (*mag.*) from the westernmost rock, which was about four miles to the south of the south Woman's Island. The weather was too thick to allow of any angles being taken. The rocks or reefs are laid down on the plans in the 'Pandora's' hydrographic book kept for that purpose. In going into Upernivik the two islands off the Hope were left on the starboard hand, and a course was shaped between them and the next one to the northward. In leaving Upernivik the 'Pandora' passed to the eastward of the Talbot Reef, which was clearly visible, and then a course was shaped to the N.W. The reef laid down off the south end of the small island on which the colony of Upernivik is situated, is visible by the break of the sea if a good look-out is kept.

observations, placing them in lat. 73° 36' N., long. 57° 47' W. There were four islands visible, lying E.N.E. and W.S.W. Snow fell until midnight. We were now deserted by every living thing.

At 9 A.M. of the 15th there was a beautiful break in the sky. The magnificent glacier was also before us, and Capes Seddon, Lewis, and Walker in sight.[1] A few huge icebergs were scattered here and there, but we saw no floe-ice. Being quite out of fresh water, we sent away a boat to one of the bergs for some loose pieces of ice. The afternoon was glorious. There was a clear, brilliant sky, and a temperature of 35°. The fog was gone, and only one or two bergs were to be seen. We had also a constant swell from the N.W. and W.N.W., and could hardly believe that we were in the dreaded Melville Bay. It was more like passing a fine autumnal night on the Atlantic. Near this point, on August 30, 1857, the 'Fox' was hampered with the ice, and finally beset altogether for a winter's drift with the pack. We reminded ourselves that it would not be wise to " halloo until out of the wood." There was, however, no prospect of meeting the middle pack ice, and we steered a direct course for Cape York. To my astonishment, the small quantity of ice we met was completely deserted, and we only saw an occasional fulmar, no looms, seals, or any living thing; and the contrast between the brilliant sun and iceless sea, with the absence of all life, was most wonderful. We could not have been far from the middle pack, as whenever the flaws of wind came from W.S.W. or S.W. the air was raw and cold, and fog with light snow, or rather frozen particles of mist, came on. Our latitude at noon was 74° 46' N., the longitude being 60° 9' W. We continued slowly through the night, with light S.W. winds, no ice being in sight except a few bergs. The barometer was 29·65 ; temperature 30° to 35° Fahr. We now had occasional calms, and used our steam,

---

[1] These capes are along the shore of Melville Bay.

going as slowly as possible to save fuel. The ship's bottom was so completely covered with long grass as to be rendered almost motionless unless in a fresh breeze, and the low temperature of the water appeared not to have the slightest effect upon it. This was a serious matter, our progress being so retarded that I feared we should not be able to advance any great distance in this season. At noon the remarkable peaked mountain to the east of Cape Melville was in sight above the mist which hung to the northward. We were now passing through another chain of grounded icebergs, and I was forcibly reminded of the time when, beset at this season of the year in the 'Fox,' we drifted past this very place, and expected to be driven against icebergs in the same positions as those now before us. Could they be the same? To me it was doubtful, although the same bergs apparently have been seen by former navigators year after year.

At five o'clock our quietude was temporarily broken into by an alarm in the ship. All hands on deck, for Joe had seen a bear swimming across our bows, and had run down for his rifle. A boat was lowered, and Lillingston and myself went away, and returned with a young she-bear about five feet long. Poor thing, she made a gallant swim for it, and it was with difficulty that we overtook her in the boat. I sent away another boat, with a small party, to shoot *rotches*, of which thousands were feeding among the ice-floes.[1]

At eight o'clock we arrived near the land in the neighbourhood of Cape York,[2] where we found quantities of smashed-up ice, enormous bergs, and small pieces. It looked as if there had been a heavy gale; but there was too much fog to see any distance towards the shore, which also seemed full of ice. Out to the W. and S.W. the sea was perfectly clear. By midnight

[1] The *Alca alle*, or little auk, called *agpaliarsuk* by the Eskimo.
[2] Named by Sir John Ross after the Duke of York, on August 16, 1818, His Royal Highness's birthday.

we had to stop steaming, owing to a thick fog and being beset
with small and thin floes, apparently of this season's formation.
The temperature fell to 28°, and the ice crystals could be seen
rapidly forming between the pieces of ice. Our rigging was
covered with a white coating of frost. I had hoped that the
low temperature in passing through the ice would have killed
the weed on the ship's bottom, but was disappointed on the
following morning to find it as flourishing as ever.

CHAPTER VI.

THE CARY ISLANDS.

WE were now about eight miles south of Cape York, and fell in with streams of ice, composed of old floes, and new ice and bergs, extending out from the land towards the S.W. for ten or fifteen miles. After passing the ice, we proceeded towards the Cary Islands, our artist taking sketches of the Beverley cliffs and the Petowak glacier. The natives come down to Cape York at this season to catch rotches in nets for their winter stock.[1] We could not, however, without serious delay, get close in to the land, to see if any natives were there, so I now steered for the Cary Islands, where I expected to find despatches from the 'Alert' and 'Discovery.' We had a fine calm night, with a light southerly air occasionally. We passed Wolstenholme Island, and at 8 A.M. sighted the south-eastern of the Cary Islands in the distance. Towards noon of the 18th of August, we were drawing near and rising the N.W. isle of the group, making, however, but slow progress, as I limited the engineers to the Waigat coal, much to their discomfiture. The wind springing up from the northward and freshening to a strong breeze, we beat up to the N.W. island, and lay-to about two miles or rather less to W.S.W.,

---

[1] We did not, in passing along the face of the Petowak glacier, experience the strong current spoken of by Inglefield ('Summer Search for Sir John Franklin,' p. 51), but in the evening we fancied we could detect a slight northerly stream, which I attributed to the flood tide. We had a constant swell, almost as if in the Atlantic. It came from N.W. and S.W., and we were even obliged to hook back the cabin doors, which one would imagine a very unusual thing in these seas in fine weather. It must indicate a large expanse of water. The barometer fluctuated but little, between 29·65 and 29·80; temperature about 25° to 30° Fahr.; surface of sea, 34° to 36°.

having to avoid a sunken rock lying about three-quarters of a mile west of the S.W. island, off the north extreme. We also observed a reef above water, with rocks extending a cable length from each end, lying a good mile west from the middle of the N.W. island.

I took the first whale-boat, and with some provisions and the two casks of letters for the 'Alert' and 'Discovery,' left the ship and sailed towards a promising bay at the mouth of a considerable river or valley on the west side of the island, and we arrived shortly on the beach, and landed without much difficulty.

I sent the boat round to another little cove about a quarter of a mile to the north-westward for safety. Lieutenant Lillingston, Lieutenant Beynen, and Mr. McGahan accompanied me. We immediately ascended towards a cairn on the summit, and after some tough travelling, and crossing a small glacier, we came to almost level ground, where we found two large cairns. Most anxiously we examined the ground with pick and shovel all round the cairn, but failed to find the slightest trace left by either the 'Alert' or the 'Discovery,' nor were there any signs of the spot having been recently visited. The result of our search merely proved that the large cairn was erected on the 17th of July, 1867, by the men of the steam whaler 'Intrepid,' Captain David Souter, a record stating that "other whale ships were in sight at the time. Little water to the N.W., weather excellent, and all well. All the ships are clean. The finder will please deposit when found. Deposited in the north side of the other cairn is a bottle of rum and some tobacco.

(Signed)   " CAPTAIN DAVID SOUTER.
              " GEO. A. CRAIG, *Surgeon.*
              " CAPTAIN J. B. WALKER, *S.S.* '*Alexander.*'
              " (VAN WATERSCHOVELT, *Surgeon.*)"

Farther on in the same paper :

"Visited on the 27th June, 1869, by Captain Walker, S.S. 'Alexander'; Captain Bruce, S.S. 'Esquimaux.' Find the liquor in good order, and very palatable. No water to be seen from the top of the island this day. All clean excepting the 'Diana,' who secured one fish in the early part of the season. All well.

> "J. B. WALKER.
> "CHAS. YULE.
> "ROBERT M. G. ANDERSON,
> "*Surgeon S.S. 'Alexander.'*

"Also signed, GEO. F. DAVIDSON, *S.S. 'Erik.'*

"Captain Jones sitting fatigued in the distance.

> "JAMES DEWARS, *Surgeon S.S. 'Esquimaux.'*
> "PETER THOMPSON, *Second Mate, 'Esquimaux.'*

"The 'Alexander,' 'Esquimaux,' 'Erik,' and 'Camperdown,' all of Dundee, fast to the ice.

> "Au revoir!"

I then examined every elevation of the island, and seeing a cairn on a small knoll at the extreme N.W., distant about three miles, I sent Lieutenant Beynen, with three men, to examine it; to signal to me if any record was discovered, and not to open anything themselves. After an absence of an hour and a half, they returned, having found nothing beyond an old record tin which had been previously opened, and was almost destroyed by rust. On it could be deciphered, in painted white letters, the following:

> "RESOLUT .
>
> and
>
> ASSISTA . . ."

The cairn had also been half pulled down, and a wooden staff which had been erected was broken in two.

Our search showed that the islands had been visited by whale ships in 1867 and 1869, and that the N.W. extremity of the N.W. island had been visited by the 'Resolute' and 'Assistance' in 1851, when under the command of Captain Austin.[1] I need scarcely express my disappointment on not finding any letter or news from the Government Expedition, as Captain Nares had written to me from Godhavn, stating his determination to leave despatches at the Cary Islands: I had gone nearly 200 miles out of my way, and consumed ten tons of coal in my endeavours to reach this point, and to carry out my promise to deliver the letters from England here.

[1] The Cary (not Carey) Islands were discovered by William Baffin on the 8th of July, 1616, and he named them after one of his patrons, Mr. Allwin Cary, of the family of Lord Hunsdon. Sir John Ross sighted them on the 20th of August, 1818. The 'Assistance' and 'Resolute,' on their return voyage, after a heavy gale of wind, sighted the Cary Islands on the 21st of August, 1851, and a cairn was observed on one of the most conspicuous heights of the N.W. island. A boat was sent to examine it, in charge of Mr. Clements Markham, then a midshipman in H.M.S. 'Assistance,' and it was found to consist of a pile of stones, with an upright piece of spruce deal 5 feet long and 5 inches broad. The letters—I—I M—R D, with the date 1827, were cut on one side, and on the other T M—D K, nearly obliterated. Fourteen whalers were to the northward of the Cary Islands in 1827, and most probably one of them left this cairn. The cairn was built up higher, and a record was deposited in the tin case discovered by the 'Pandora,' in August, 1875.

The Cary Islands are in 76° 45′ N., and 72° 50′ W. Five of them are from a mile and a half to two miles in diameter, three smaller, besides detached rocks. The formation is gneiss, rising to a height of 400 feet above the sea, and there is a rich growth of *Cochlearia Grœnlandica*, and other Arctic plants. The cliffs are breeding places for looms, dovekeys, and rotches, of which the officers of the 'Assistance' shot 900 during August 22. Mr. Markham also found ancient remains of Eskimos, consisting of stone huts, cachés, graves, and a stone fox-trap. (See an account of the Cary Islands at p. 335 of the 'Aurora Borealis,' the Arctic newspaper issued on board H.M.S. 'Assistance' in 1850–51, and published by Colburn and Co. in 1852.)

Great care ought to be taken in approaching the N.W. or largest of the Cary Islands, as several sunken rocks lie to the westward of it, and the current of the tide runs strong in the flood to the northward, rendering it necessary to give any grounded icebergs a wide berth. As far as could be judged by the shore, it was high water on the 18th of August, two days after the full moon, at 11 P.M. A good landing will be found, with northerly to easterly winds, on the west side of the N.W. island, at the mouth of a deep ravine, in which is a river, and a quarter of a mile to the northward of which is a little cove with a beach, upon which a boat can be hauled up.

Having carefully examined all round, and failing to find any other cairn, I wrote to Captain Nares, or the Commanding Officer H.M.S. 'Alert' or 'Discovery,' stating that the letters contained in two water-tight casks would be found on a knoll above the beach, close to the mouth of the wide river or valley on the west side of the island, and bearing about S.W. from the cairn on the summit. It was now blowing hard from the northward, and was bitterly cold; we had been six hours on the island, so I hastily packed up and descended to the shore, and having carried the casks to the top of the knoll, about seventy to eighty feet above the sea, we deposited them, built a cairn to indicate their position, and tied a comforter to a staff made of one of the boat's stretchers. The casks are well above all chance of the sea ever coming over them, and can easily be found by the directions given in my notice on the summit of the island.

It was now past midnight, and as we could do no more for our fellow-voyagers, we re-embarked for the ship.

I rapidly turned over in my mind the nature of our situation. If I had had news from Captain Nares stating that he had gone on positively, I should have decided to beat up to Littleton Island, and take the letters on. But in the face of a northern gale, the season fast passing away, and no information as to where the 'Alert' and 'Discovery' had gone, I considered it far best to leave things as they were and proceed on my own affairs, as, if it were possible by chance that the ships were still southward of us, they would pick up their letters on the way, and if north they would probably send down in the spring for them, if considered of sufficient consequence.

To have gone northward under this uncertainty would have involved my giving up all idea of Lancaster Sound, so I determined to make the best of my way in continuation of our programme, and at 1 A.M. we bore up before a fresh N.N.W. gale, with a high sea which rolled in on both

D

sides of our decks, compelling us to secure the bunker-lids. Not a particle of ice was in sight, excepting a few gigantic bergs aground against the islands, and on the distant horizon. The engines were stopped, and we flew before the breeze to the S.W. at a speed which was quite new to us, and with the first really fair wind since leaving England.

CHAPTER VII.

LANCASTER SOUND AND BARROW STRAIT.

THE fair wind fell off as we sighted the land of North Lincoln and Coburg Island, and we had a moderate N.W. wind through the night, with fine weather. We fell in with ice on the morning of the 20th of August, lying about thirty miles east of Cape Horsburgh and Philpot's Island, and the wind coming from the southward we tacked to the S.E. A thick fog came on shortly afterwards, so we continued to the S.E. until evening, when it lifted, and we saw ice extending out from the land in small and large floes, intermingled with bergs.

Three bears being seen on the ice, I went away in the second cutter with Pirie and Beynen, and after shooting the old she-bear and one cub we succeeded in getting a rope round the larger cub and towing him to the ship. Now began a most lively scene. The bear was almost full grown, and it was with some difficulty we got him on board and tied down to ring-bolts with his hind legs secured; and notwithstanding this rough treatment he showed most wonderful energy in trying to attack anyone who came within reach, and especially our dogs, who seemed to delight in trying his temper. He was at last secured on the quarter-deck with a chain round his neck and under his fore-arms, and soon began to feed ravenously on—I am sorry to have to write it—his own mother, who was speedily cut up and pieces of her flesh thrown to my new shipmate. I hoped that he was only an adopted child, and the great difference between him and the other cub warranted this supposition, as, being three times the size of the other, he could not have been of the same litter.

On the 21st we steered on towards the land about Cape Horsburgh; a considerable quantity of ice lying off this remarkable promontory, or rather point, the glacier running down until almost to the sea-level, and projecting out over the low land. There is a singular conical hill to the northward of this glacier, which appears from the sea to be almost isolated. Passing round the floating ice, and grounded pieces, we saw several seals basking in the sun, and, going away with Lillingston and Beynen, I brought on board a large bearded one,[1] which we shot upon a high floe-piece. In towing him off he revived, broke the rope, and disappeared, but shortly afterwards arose, quite dead.

On approaching Cape Warrender,[2] a dense fog came on, and at 10 P.M. I was suddenly called on deck, and found the ship running amongst floes of ice. We immediately backed out, and stood away to the southward, when the fog lifted for a few minutes, and we saw a close pack extending across the straits as far as was visible from the topmast head. It was a dismal night, dense fog, freezing hard, a cutting wind, and surrounded by floes. I attempted to make fast, but the currents so twisted the floes, that we only increased the risk of being beset; I therefore continued working out to the eastward the whole night, never leaving the deck.

At four in the morning of the 22nd, the fog cleared off, revealing exactly what I had so much feared; a perfect barrier of ice, extending from Cape Warrender right across the straits; at least, as far as we could see from aloft, and filling Croker Bay[3] right into the land. We had also ice to the eastward, but seeing a lane of water, I stood in to the

[1] The bearded seal (*Phoca barbata*) is the *ursuk* of the Eskimo. It is the largest species next to the walrus.

[2] Cape Warrender, so named by Sir John Ross in 1818, is at the north side of the entrance of Lancaster Sound.

[3] Croker Bay is on the north shore of Lancaster Sound, west of Cape Warrender. It was so named by Parry in 1819, to compensate for the Croker Mountains which Sir John Ross placed across Lancaster Sound in 1818, and which had to be expunged.

northward, in hopes of finding a lead inshore in Croker Bay. By 4 P.M. we were completely stopped, and made fast to a heavy floe, about eight or ten miles off Cape Warrender. This floe was of immense size, extending right into the land, not a drop of water being seen between us and the shore. At seven o'clock we were being surrounded, so I hastily cast off and stood back into the open space through which we had come, and into the middle of the straits. We had divine service in the evening; and unable to see any way of proceeding, I ordered the ship to be hove-to, and went to take a little rest, the first for thirty-six hours.

Our new shipmate, the bear, made desperate struggles to get over the rail into the sea, but the chain was tightened, and at last he went to sleep.

The 23rd was a bright, warm day. Joe had shot a small seal. We lived on seal and bear (of which we had about 600 lb. hung up in the rigging), preferring it to the ship's provisions. Not an opening was to be seen in the ice. We were about in the middle of the straits, and having yesterday made the north shore, now steered over to the south coast, and entering a slack place in the pack, we were enabled, after much thumping and some intricate steering, to force our way through the floes and new ice, and reach a clear water off Admiralty Inlet.[1] We made fast to a berg-piece, in order to get fresh-water ice, but soon found a very strong current, and were towed back to the E.N.E., towards the pack from which we had emerged, compelling us to cast off before we had completed watering. I was at a loss to account for the barrier across Lancaster Sound, never having heard of a record of any similar pack at this season in this part of the straits. Most of the floes were large and quite fresh, the snow apparently remaining just as it had fallen in the winter.

[1] Admiralty Inlet is on the south side of Lancaster Sound, opposite to Croker Bay.

Could the pack have driven out of Admiralty Inlet? or had the straits in this longitude not broken up at all this season? I hoped later to receive reports from the whalers on these points.

Admiralty Inlet was now before us. It is a wide strait, and was apparently open, although from aloft a line of ice was reported on the distant horizon. I was sorely tempted to proceed down the inlet and communicate with the natives, with the object of ascertaining if it led through into Regent Inlet as I believed, but this report of ice precluded the attempt; and, moreover, we saw a dark sky in the westward off Cape Craufurd,[1] and, therefore, pushed on along the edge of the pack, soon coming to an open sea, with the pack receding to the northward, in the direction of Cape Bullen. The weather began to threaten, and the barometer fell rapidly, and E. to S.E. winds springing up and freshening, we bowled away to the westward, in the direction of Cape Craufurd, with far lighter hearts than yesterday, when our progress seemed to be entirely barred. While at tea we heard a loud crash, and hastening on deck found that we had just grazed an iceberg, which had broken our starboard anchor adrift. Had the ship not answered her helm readily, we must have hit it, and in all probability the ' Pandora's ' career would have been ended for ever. The night promised to be gloomy, and I was somewhat anxious: snow fell thickly at 8 P.M., with a gusty S.E. wind. We proceeded with easy steam, ready to put about at any moment. The temperature was only 30°, but the wind was soft and mild. As I anticipated, we passed a most dismal night, the wind increasing and howling in the rigging. Snow and sleet also prevailed as we scudded onward, an iceblink frequently ahead; then the inevitable floe in streams and

---

[1] Cape Craufurd is on the western side of the entrance to Admiralty Inlet. It was so named by Parry, on the 30th of August, 1820, after his friend Mr. William Petrie Craufurd.

loose pieces, with the sea dashing over them as we flew between. Now and then the moon shone out, but only to make the scene still more ghastly, for our masts and rigging, decks and bulwarks were covered with ice and snow. At 11 P.M. we caught a glimpse of the land, apparently some-where between Sargent Point and Cape York.[1] It was only for a moment, and then all was darkness and wind and snow and ice. While we were in this situation our bear gradually worked himself into a state of frantic excitement—getting up to the rail, watching the floe-ice rapidly dashing past our side —and in his attempts to get over the bulwarks he released his chain until it was evident that in a few moments he would be free, whether to dive overboard or to run a muck among the watch appeared a question of doubt. The alarm being given by Pirie, who was writing up the deck log, the watch was called to secure the bear, and I fear that during the half hour which elapsed the ship was left, more or less, to take care of herself. The whole watch, besides Pirie with a revolver, and myself with a crowbar, assaulted the unfortunate Bruin, whose frantic struggles and endeavours to attack everyone within reach were quite as much as we could control. He was loose, but by a fortunate event a running noose was passed round his neck, and the poor brute was hauled down to a ring-bolt until we could secure the chain round his neck and body. I had hitherto no conception of the strength of these animals, and especially of the power of their jaws. Fearing that the iron crowbar might injure his teeth, I jammed a mop handle into his mouth while the others were securing his chain, and he bit it completely through. At last Bruin gave in, and beyond an occasional struggle to get loose, and a constant low growling,

---

[1] So named by Sir Edward Parry in 1819, after the Duke of York. It is at the western entrance of Prince Regent Inlet. Parry named another cape, between Admiralty and Navy Board Inlets, on August 31, 1820, after the Right Hon. Charles P. Yorke, grandson of the first Earl of Hardwicke, who was First Lord of the Admiralty from 1810 to 1812.

he gave us no further trouble. I ought to mention that in the midst of the scrimmage the Doctor was called up to give him a dose of opium, in the hope of subduing him by this means; but having succeeded in getting him to swallow a piece of blubber saturated with chloroform and opium sufficient to kill a dozen men, our Bruin did not appear to have experienced the slightest effect, and the Doctor, who volunteered to remain up, and expressed some anxiety as to the bear's fate, retired below somewhat disappointed.

The snow turned into sleet in the morning, and we scudded up Barrow Strait, and at eight suddenly saw land. Our compasses were almost useless. We had been threading through the ice. We could not distinguish anything beyond a dark black foot of cliff, about two miles away. The ship was put about, and stood to the S.E. Gradually the fog and sleet were less dense, and we saw by the trend of the coast line that we were on the north shore, for I cannot say that at first I did not feel sure we were close down upon Leopold Island. On the fog again lifting, we saw about ten miles of coast about Cape Fellfoot, and at 10 A.M. bore away to the westward again, before a strong easterly wind, passing through streams of heavy ice, which was much broken by the gale of the previous night. We did not feel the full effects of this gale, being sheltered by the pack we passed through. I recollect that in the 'Fox' we were subjected to a much more severe gale when running up the same straits under similar circumstances, with the exception of having twenty or thirty miles of pack ice between us and Baffin's Bay.

The barometer fell to 29·40. We got occasional glimpses of the land until 4 P.M., when all was obscured by a perfect pall of fog. I kept the ship S.W. as we passed what must have been Maxwell Bay, the wind still blowing in gusts from the eastward, and heavy ice coming constantly in our way. Looms were continually flying out to seaward, and occasionally a flock would cross us, evidently making straight into the land, and by these signs and the wind we continued our lonely course, our compasses being useless, and there being no other guide. A dense gloom and fog, with snow and sleet, prevailed throughout the night, and we could see but a few cables' length, the mist hanging over us like a curtain. I was anxious to get to Beechey Island, to examine the state of the depôt there in case of a mishap, and at 5 A.M., on the 25th, we rounded to, after passing through a heavy stream of ice, not being able to determine our position. We had no sun and no soundings, and I could only judge that we were somewhere off the land about Cape Hurd. This was a dark day, with nothing to distract the attention from the damp, cold, and gloom, beyond the occasional trimming of the sails. We were iced-up aloft, and great flakes of frozen snow and hard pieces of ice frequently came down. I earnestly watched the barometer, and at 6 P.M. the mercury rose one-tenth of an inch, and the wind, which was squally and baffling from the eastward, veered more to the N.E. The looms began to pass us from the north, flying south, and at 1.30 P.M. we caught sight of a patch of snow at the foot of the land, which suddenly appeared as if it had rolled from the heavens, and was not more than half a mile distant. We were off Cape Ricketts, and a magnificent view was displayed before us. The steep, precipitous cliffs appeared to hang over our heads, and all the clefts and ravines and gorges in the neighbourhood were white with drift snow. Cape Hotham[1] appeared in the distance like a golden mound, the sun being reflected upon its icy summit. No ice could be seen, save a few half-worn bergs, one of which supplied us with enough water for a week's consumption in less than half an hour, its edges being broken off with an axe. White whales and seals swam around, and appeared to gaze at us as if we

[1] The S.E. point of Cornwallis Island, forming the western entrance to Wellington Channel. Parry described it as like two boats turned bottom up.

were some apparition coming out from the gloom, and we
seemed to be in another world.   Such are the changes in this
extraordinary climate.   The contrast between the shining sun
above, and our sloppy, half-frozen decks and snow-covered
rigging was most striking.

CHAPTER VIII.

BEECHEY ISLAND.[1]

WE lighted our stoves below, for the first time since leaving England, giving our damp and cold quarters a good drying up, and raising the temperature below from 38° to 54°, a heat which really felt oppressive. At 8 P.M. we were flying towards Beechey, under steam and fore-and-aft canvas. We attempted to take photographs, and occasionally stopped the ship, but our artist desponded in consequence of the slight movement of the waters, which appeared to us only the merest undulation. He succeeded, however, in getting one or two of the magnificent headlands, as we stopped for the purpose immediately under them. We also tried the lead-line, but could find no bottom at 70 fathoms, close to the shore; there may be from 90 to 100 fathoms, as the lead had been down twice on a hard ground with 120 fathoms out. At 9.30 we sighted Cape Riley and Beechey Island. We saw a cairn with a staff at the south end, and we soon made out a house and boats upon the low shore. The wind increased from the north, with all appearance of a gale. I prepared to anchor, and steered in towards the bay. At eleven we anchored in 12 fathoms, mud and clay bottom, Northumberland House bearing N.N.E. (*mag.*) about a quarter of a mile, and veered to 30 fathoms of cable. It now blew a gale from N. to N.N.W. directly out of the bay. I went on shore with two of the officers to inspect the place, and ascertain the state of the provisions and boats. I found that

---

[1] Lieutenant Beechey, the First Lieutenant of the 'Hecla,' made this land to be an island on the 22nd of August, 1819, and Parry named it out of respect for Sir William Beechey.

the house had been stove in at the door and in both sides by the wind and bears, and almost everything light and movable either blown out or dragged out by bears, which had also torn up all the tops of the bales, and scattered the contents around for some distance. The house was nearly full of ice and snow, and frozen so hard that we could not remove anything excepting with pickaxe and crowbar, and even then only the few things which were projecting above the surface. The tea-chests were all broken open, and most of their contents scattered about. Many of the beef casks had been eaten through the bilges, and the contents extracted. The whole place was a scene of confusion, and the kitchen a mere wreck. I could not find any traces of the place having been visited by human beings since our departure in the ' Fox,' on the 14th of August, 1858. The only thing I noticed was that a coal fire had been made on the beach; but this might have been done by our crew of the ' Fox,' or even by the crews of the squadron of Sir Edward Belcher. A cask of rum standing in the door-way intact was conclusive proof to my mind that neither Eskimo nor British sailors had entered that way.

I found the ' Mary,' cutter yacht, in good condition; her bottom appeared quite uninjured, but we could not see her garboard for the stones heaped under the bilges to keep her upright. She stood in apparently the same position as when formerly placed there. In her fore compartment is an anchor and chain, some horn lanterns as bright as new, and sundry boatswain's stores. In her main cabin the sails are stowed in the wings, and beyond a slight leakage from the decks the cabin was dry, perfectly clean, and free of snow. The after compartment was in a similarly good state, and a set of carpenter's tools and caulking implements were carefully stowed there. The ladder was in excellent order, most of the spars good. Standing rigging was aloft, but no running gear could be found. I should consider that the ' Mary ' might be made available for a retreating party in about four or five days with the resources of Northumberland House.[1] The lifeboat cutter lying by her was marked

↑
X X X
W
N—1150
Oct.
1851.

She was in fair condition, and only required the wood ends to be refastened. Her oars and masts were complete, but her sails were partially torn by bears. There were ten copper crutches in her fore and after compartments.

She could be made serviceable in one day. A lifeboat cutter near the house was next examined. She was lying end on to the beach, above high-water mark, and is marked

↑
X X X
W
N—1151
Octo
1851.

She also was in good condition, and only required re-fastening and caulking. There were ten brass crutches in the compartments, and the oars and masts were in and outside the house. The sails were not seen, but were supposed to have been torn up by the bears. This boat could also be made serviceable in one day, and is in an easy position for launching.

---

[1] Northumberland House on Beechey Island, named after the then First Lord of the Admiralty, was built by Commander (now Rear-Admiral) Pullen when in command of the 'North Star,' which ship wintered there in 1852–53 and 1853–54, as a depôt for Sir Edward Belcher's expedition. The house was built in the autumn of 1852, of lower masts and spars taken from the American whaler 'M'Lellan,' which was crushed by the ice in Melville Bay in 1852. Sir Leopold M'Clintock visited the house and examined the stores on the 11th of August, 1858.

A whale-boat on the south side of the house was unserviceable. The ice-boat on runners could be easily made serviceable. The flagstaff was standing all right, and the arrangement for pointing the direction was in good order, but there was no vane or arrow.

I found the pedestal in good condition, and also the marble tablet in memory of the Franklin expedition, the brass plate which M'Clintock fastened on it being quite bright, as if the bears had been lying on it.[1] The record box was hanging to a beam in the house, and having examined the original list of provisions, and M'Clintock's record, which was as fresh as if just written, I took a copy of it, and removed all the documents to the post office in the pedestal, for safer keeping, in which I only found a memorandum from Sir E. Belcher.

At eight in the morning of the 26th, the wind having partially moderated, we began to clear away some of the ice and snow; and having with great difficulty found such provisions as we were actually in need of, and thirteen bags of coal, of which there still remained at least ten tons, I placed a record of our proceedings in the pedestal, with a list of the provisions taken away, and embarked at 7 P.M., having carefully repaired and closed the house. Our artist was busily employed all day in taking photographs of every object of interest, and Mr. Beynen was sent to the summit of the island to report on the ice. He could see none from any visible point in the horizon, but in the south-west a mist was hanging which prevented the completion of his observations.

[1] See M'Clintock's 'Fate of Franklin,' p. 173.

NORTHUMBERLAND HOUSE, BEECHY ISLAND.

CHAPTER IX.

PEEL STRAIT.

HAVING got all the boats up, we weighed anchor at 8 P.M., and stood away to the southward for Peel Strait, the wind being fresh from the N.W. At four next morning we were among loose ice, and at noon a heavy pack stopped our progress, when I made fast to a floe to await the clearing of the fog, which soon lifted, enabling us to proceed under steam through the pack, which extended as far as we could see along the north shore of North Somerset, and particularly off Cape Rennell and about half-way across Barrow Strait, lying in an easterly and westerly direction. As we pushed on, the ice became more open, and by 5 P.M. we were steering through navigable lanes towards Limestone Island, which we could just see from aloft, topping above the icy horizon. We were off Cunningham Inlet, and Cape Hotham,[1] with Griffith Island[2] in sight, to the northward. We ranged up to an enormous "ursuk" (bearded seal), nearly as large as a walrus, for which we at first took him; but he was lying on a very small piece of ice, and although our bullets went through him, he floundered into the sea, and did not rise again. We thus lost at least 500 lb. of good meat and oil.

Our bear was getting more reconciled to his confinement; but when we were among close ice, he got into a state of fury

---

[1] Cunningham Inlet is on the coast of North Somerset. Cape Hotham is the S.E. point of Cornwallis Island, forming the western side of the entrance to Wellington Channel.

[2] The expedition of Captain Austin, consisting of the 'Resolute,' 'Assistance,' 'Pioneer,' and 'Intrepid,' wintered off Griffith Island in 1850–51.

in his endeavour to get out of the ship, and our dogs were constantly worrying him by stealing his food.

At night we came to a solid barrier of ice, extending out
from the land about Cape Rennell to the W.N.W., as far as
could be seen from aloft, with a bright icy sky from south
round to N.W. We then made fast to await a change.[1] I
determined to wait at least twenty-four hours, and if we could
not then pass, to bear up for Regent Inlet and Bellot Strait;
but at eight in the morning of the 28th of August the ice
slackened a little, and by ten we pushed through a small lane
which ultimately led us to Limestone Island.[2]

Our artist took more photographs and sketches while we
were fast to the floe, and we took the same opportunity to fill
up with fresh water, and give the dogs a run.

This morning it was freezing hard, with a temperature of
27°, and our rigging was completely covered with rime; but
dark clouds now arose in the south-west, the barometer began
to fall, and the wind to arise from the eastward to E.S.E.
Finding a land water round Limestone Island, I hauled into
the N.E. entrance, and landed to examine the stores which
were said to be at Cape Bunny. It was raining heavily, with
gusts from the mainland, and occasional sleet. I landed, and
hauled up our boat on a shelving beach composed entirely of
loose limestone pebbles, and at once proceeded to the low
point (Cape Bunny), but could not find anything. Having
sent the Doctor and Beynen round the beach, I ascended the
gradual slope or ridge leading to the summit of the island, and

---

[1] We sounded in 110 fathoms while fast to the floe, bottom limestone mud, about
seven miles off the land, Cunningham Inlet, E.S.E. (*true*). Before the change in the
weather, the red sandstone hills about Cape Anne (on the mainland of North Somerset,
opposite Limestone Island) presented a brilliant reddish glow from the reflection of the
sun, and reminded me of the Highlands when the heather is in full bloom on a bright
day. On the other hand, the transition to the limestone was clearly defined, the latter
presenting the usual dull and gloomy appearance so well known to Arctic travellers.

[2] Limestone Island is on the east side of the entrance to Peel Strait.

when about three-quarters of a mile from the point, and at an elevation of about 300 feet, I descried a cairn, evidently built by civilized hands, the ground having been excavated to form the base, and the top being composed of loose stones. Much to my disappointment, we dug up this cairn without finding anything, and I cannot conjecture by whom it was built, or for what purpose. I then mounted to the top of the island on the south face, an elevation of 600 feet by aneroid, but the squalls of wind and rain prevented my getting a good view of the sea. I noticed, however, that the main pack had already moved off from the land to a distance of about three miles, but that it still extended round in a southerly or S.S.W. direction until shut in by the land against Cape Pressure. As I descended the rain came down in torrents, and we found it cold work rebuilding the cairn, to which we added some large stones to make it conspicuous, and having searched the ground all round, and especially on the magnetic north side, without success, I deposited a record in a tin box. I cannot think why we could not find the provisions. I had always supposed that there is but one Cape Bunny, and that it was here that the stores were landed, but there were certainly none to be found on the island.[1]

---

[1] In the spring of 1854, when it was unknown whether parties from the 'Enterprise,' under Captain Collinson, might not make their way up Peel Strait from the westward, Sir Edward Belcher ordered two officers, with sledges, to go to Cape Bunny, on Limestone Island, and deposit a depôt there, in case any parties from the 'Enterprise' should come that way.

Mr. Herbert, a mate of H.M.S. 'Assistance,' left the 'North Star' at Beechey Island, crossed Barrow Strait on the ice, and reached Limestone Island on April 1, 1854. He buried a depôt, consisting of 370 rations of bread, pemmican, bacon, and rum, and 473 of all other stores, on a spit at the eastern extreme of the island, covering it high up with shingle. He also left a flag and staff with a cylinder attached, containing a notice. Mr. Herbert returned to the 'North Star' on April 9.

On April 3 Mr. Shellabeer, the second master of the 'North Star,' arrived at Limestone Island with a second depôt, consisting of 396 rations of small stores, 436 of rum, and 296 of biscuit and meats. He deposited these stores with Mr. Herbert's depôt at Cape Bunny, built a cairn on the high part of the spit of the island, and left a bamboo on it, also depositing a notice. He left a list of the stores in a cairn over the depôt. Mr. Shellabeer returned to the 'North Star' on April 11.

*

The Doctor having reported that he had found remains of ancient Eskimos, I proceeded towards the beach on the south of the island, and saw immediately under the precipitous cliffs which shelter the spot from the north winds, about ten circular rings of unusually heavy stones, which had formed the foundation of summer tents, also several cachés made of heavy stones, oblong, and floored with flat cakes of limestone. Quantities of bones of the seal, walrus, and whale were lying about, but we saw no other relics except what appeared to be a piece of charred coal, which I took on board.

During our absence, the man left in charge of the boat saw a seal crawl up on the shore close to him ; but, notwithstanding that he had a revolver and ammunition, it is almost needless to say that he did not get it. We noticed the tide ebbing from the time we landed at 3.30 until we re-embarked at 5.30, when it was apparently nearly low water by the shore, the current having continued running about three knots to the northward through the channel between the island and the main.

I embarked with an anxious mind, for the wind was increasing to a gale, the weather thickening fast; we were drenched with rain and very cold, and the prospect from the top of the island was not very encouraging. However, I was determined to persevere, and to push into Peel Strait if possible. I ordered the ship to be steered through the channel between the island and the main, and having changed my clothes in our snug and warm cabin, I went on the damp, dreary deck again. We passed through the channel, sounding in thirty fathoms, about a quarter of a mile off the extreme point of Cape Bunny, and finding a strong current running through from the southward. The night was one of the most dreary I ever passed at sea, and I have had my share. The wind continued in fitful gusts, rain and sleet in torrents, thick mist, no soundings, no compass, land on one side and ice on the other. We could just distinguish the foot of the land and cliffs, as we passed close under them, by the dark line over the gleam of the grounded ice. By nine it was dark. We furled all sails, and steamed against the gale, edging off to the ice as a more secure guide for our course than the land, which we could not follow. By eleven it was so thick that we could literally see nothing but the occasional sheen of the ice as we passed along it on the starboard hand. Anxiously I waited for light; but it was three o'clock in the morning of the 29th before we could fairly see, and at about four a lift in the mist enabled us to see that we were off Cape Granite,[1] and steering a fair course along the land. By seven we were off a wide bay, the land receding from about ten miles south of Cape Granite, with a fringe of islands north and south, and forming the line of coast. Our patent log was put over, and on the mist clearing in the westward we saw the land to the W.N.W., about Lyons Point and Cape Biggs.[2] The wind had now come round to W.S.W. and west, but as yet we saw no sun to guide us, or by which to take any angles or directions; so we continued along the coast line, the ice receding, and there being none visible in the W.S.W. or south. The barometer rose to 29·95, with an appearance of better weather, and we seemed to have arrived in another climate, and also in an iceless sea, for the cold sting was gone from the air. The land was quite exposed and devoid of snow, excepting occasionally in the interior, in which direction we sometimes got a glimpse of snow patches.

We did not see the small island marked on the chart in the middle of the strait. By 2 P.M. we had passed Howe Harbour, and were off a projecting point not named by Sir James Ross, and which he merely noticed as having a lake upon it. Passing

---

[1] Cape Granite, on the eastern shore of Peel Strait.

[2] Lyons Point, on Prince of Wales' Island, is on the west side of the entrance to Peel Strait. Cape Biggs is on the same side, a few miles farther south.

within half a mile, we tried for soundings, but could find no
bottom with 120 fathoms. I supposed this to be Hummock
Point, and noticed a rookery of skuas[1] on the face of the
granite cliffs—they were sitting on the rocks in hundreds.
The vegetation formed an extensive green patch, extending from
near the summit to high-water mark, or where the ice forms.
We kept a good look-out on the shore by means of a powerful
astronomical telescope, and cairns were frequently reported to
me; but on inspection they proved to be granite boulder
stones, with which the coast, and especially the ridges, are
strewn.

At 10 P.M. I returned on board from visiting the cairn
built by Sir James Ross and Sir L. M'Clintock on Cape
Coulman. We found it without difficulty, as we passed close
along the coast from point to point. Landing on a small piece
of ice, we ascended to about 150 feet, and found the copper
cylinder containing the following record :—

"The cylinder which contains this paper was left here by a party detached
from Her Majesty's ships 'Enterprise' and 'Investigator,' under the command
of Captain Sir James C. Ross, Royal Navy, in search of the expedition of Sir
John Franklin, and to inform any of his party that may find it that those
ships, having wintered at Port Leopold, in long. 90° W., lat. 73° 52' N., have
formed there a depôt of provisions for the use of Sir John Franklin's party
sufficient for six months; also two very small depôts about fifteen miles south of
Cape Clarence and twelve miles south of Cape Seppings. The party are now
about to return to the ships, which, as early as possible in the spring, will push
forward to Melville Island, and search the north coast of Barrow Strait, and,
failing to meet the party they are seeking, will touch at Port Leopold on their
way back, and then return to England before the winter shall set in.

"JAMES C. ROSS, *Captain.*

"7th June, 1849."

This simple paper, left as the record of a mere visit to
the spot, really shows what a remarkable journey Ross and

---

[1] The most common skua in the Arctic regions is the *Catharacta parasitica* (or
Stercorarius parasiticus), mentioned by Fabricius, and by Crantz, i. p. 86, the *Isingak*
of the Eskimos.

M'Clintock made when they travelled on foot from Port Leopold round this unknown coast, in the days when sledge travelling was in its infancy.

It contains no claims to the discovery of Peel Strait, nor any mention as to the state of the ice or land to the southward; and although a doubt appears to have existed in the minds of the travellers as to whether it was really a strait or not, yet they seem to have preferred to leave the question doubtful rather than mislead any future voyager.

It also shows how strange are the chances of Arctic navigation, for Ross was in the exact track of the 'Erebus' and 'Terror,' and but one season after those ships were abandoned, and yet Ross's impression must have been strongly against the probability of Franklin having passed down the strait, otherwise he would have expressed his intention to follow this route with his ships in the ensuing summer, rather than the north shore of Barrow Strait.

It was in 1859, in the month of June, that, having completed the journey round the south-west coast of Prince of Wales' Land, I again started from the 'Fox' and reached Browne's[1] farthest on the north-west side of these straits, and thence, in crossing over to this eastern shore, I met with so much water on the ice that I was prevented from reaching Ross's Cairn, passing about four miles southward of it. I returned to the ship with the greatest difficulty, having found the ice between this point (Cape Coulman) and Bellot Strait flooded with water to such an extent that we were travelling knee-deep in it, and almost floating the sledge itself. I thus missed seeing the cairn, but I claim to have discovered, under M'Clintock's command, the land on both sides of these straits southward of Browne's farthest on the western shore, and

---

[1] Lieutenant Browne was the Second Lieutenant of the 'Resolute,' under Captain Austin. He led an extended sledge party from Cape Walker down the western side of Peel Strait in the spring of 1851.

southward of the point or cape about eight miles south of this cairn on the western side, and to which point Ross walked.

We saw a number of white whales in the bay immediately south of Cape Coulman, and also picked up several horns of the reindeer. Having left a copy of Ross's record with another of our own, I took away the original paper, and after carefully closing the cylinder, deposited it in its former place, and we returned to our ship, and steamed towards the next cape, distant about eight or nine miles to the southward, and the wind being southerly and the flood tide against us, we went slowly, with all sails furled.

We passed Four River Point about 10 P.M., and, a thick fog coming on, had to lay-to for the remainder of the night. At 5 A.M. we passed outside the islands lying off the coast, and found a wide stream of ice extending east and west across the strait, passing through which we came again into a large expanse of water. But an icy sky southward, and a chilly feeling in the air, warned us that we were approaching a large body of ice, and by 4 P.M. we came to the pack edge, about a mile to the northward of Levesque Island, and extending from the shore four miles north of False Inlet, or Fitzroy Inlet, in a concave form, round to the western shore. From the masthead we could see nothing to the southward but a solid pack, and a bright icy sky beyond, and a solitary iceberg about ten miles south of us, for which I could not account as it is foreign to these straits, and must either have been driven down Barrow Strait or M'Clintock Channel from the northwest. This berg was important, as bearing upon the movement of the ice here.

ICE BARRIER ACROSS PEEL STRAITS.

CHAPTER X.

AN IMPASSABLE BARRIER.

It was with a heavy heart that I made fast to the floe, about a mile and a half from shore. We were in lat. 72° 14', and close to my former encampment when travelling in June, 1859, from the 'Fox,' then in Port Kennedy. Islands, coast, and ice appeared familiar to me, and I could recognize all the points of interest which we observed during that dreadful march, when, wading up to our thighs in water, and nearly broken down with the fatigues of three months' continuous travel, I barely reached the western entrance of Bellot Strait. I can now account for our having then passed Ross's Cairn without seeing it. for it is not built upon the upper ridge of the point, and is quite concealed from view from the south, and upon almost every bearing. On the former occasion we were pressing on for our lives, and having passed Cape Coulman without distinguishing the cairn in the misty weather, it was utterly impossible to return even a yard.

By seven o'clock the 'Pandora' entered upon the scene of my former surveys in 1859, and, with some interest, combined with anxiety, my own chart was brought out for our guidance, and for corroboration, and I was surprised, considering the extremely difficult circumstances under which I was then travelling, to find how correctly the islands, and also the mainland, were laid down. We made such corrections as were found necessary, and these have enabled us to give a tolerably correct plan of these straits.

We were not allowed to enjoy much repose, for at 8 P.M.

*

the loose ice through which we had passed in the forenoon
began to settle down on us, and we were compelled to cast off
from the beach, and steam again to the northward into clear
water to escape being beset. We saw Cape Bird,[1] distant
about ten miles, and the ice appeared to be jammed into the
shore as close or even tighter than off Fitzroy Inlet, where we
were. We sounded in ninety-three fathoms, finding a sandy
bottom.

We lay-to the whole night, off the pack edge; a dense fog
set in at midnight, lasting until 5 A.M. of the 31st, when we
discovered that we had drifted close to Roquette Islands,
and I landed upon the largest of the four to deposit a record
and view the ice, getting with difficulty through the young and
loose ice which was forming between the floes.

From the summit of the island, 200 feet high, we could see
one unbroken pack extending from shore to shore, and as far
as the visible horizon to the southward, and so close that no
ship could penetrate beyond a few lengths into it. The ice
had also drifted, during the last twenty-four hours, up both
shores to northward, and we were in a deep bight, to get out
of which we should have to retire as far as Barth Island. We
could plainly see the entrance to Bellot Strait, but the ice was
closely packed on the shore, holding out no hopes of our being
able to proceed in that direction, or I should have been glad
to have held on there upon the chance of some change taking
place. Our prospect was gloomy in the extreme. I was loth
to turn back, yet there was nothing else to be done, for even
a boat could not get through this pack. We built a conspicuous cairn on the summit of the largest island, placing in it a
record, and descended to the boat. We observed the magnetic
dip to be 88° 30′.

---

[1] Cape Bird, the farthest point seen by Sir James Ross from Cape Coulman, is on the
north side of the western entrance to Bellot Strait.

We again lay-to all night, a mile or two from Roquette Islands, and in the bight of the pack, which now extended northward along the shore of North Somerset nearly to Barth Island, and westward to about the same latitude, the surface of the sea freezing all night, and presenting in the morning a glazed appearance all round. A fog commenced about 1 A.M., and at two was quite dense until eight, when I stood back to Roquette Islands. The wind remained southerly throughout the day, with intermittent fogs, and I made several preparations to land on the island to obtain another view of the ice, but it was not until 6 P.M. that we could get through the loose ice surrounding it. A strong south wind was blowing on the other side of the island, and the ice was rapidly sailing past the group. I had therefore only time to run up to the top and get a hasty glance to the south before I found it necessary to make all haste to the boat and push off to the ship, which was already surrounded by floes, and nearly cut off from us. We at once began to free ourselves from the pack, and steamed northward for about three miles, when we again lay-to.

I had observed no change from the island, and I could see no water beyond a few cracks in the first five miles. The ice had gradually crept up the shore, reaching nearly to Barth Island, and to the westward, still farther north. We were still in a deep bay in the ice. All to the southward was one unbroken pack across from side to side. I was most anxious about our position, and wished if possible to reach Bellot Strait, because there we could have held on and awaited any ice movement northward, and perhaps proceed southward after it had passed; but from this point we must inevitably have been carried northward if the pack continued to advance in that direction. Even if I had desired to winter here it would have been useless, as we could not possibly have done more than M'Clintock and Hobson did by travelling over King

William Island with the spring and winter snow on the
ground; and, moreover, we must have abandoned the ship
in the following spring before the water made on the floe,
which would render sledge travelling very difficult, and we
could not depend upon getting the ship out next summer. We
had not many hours to make up our minds, but I was inclined
to give it another day's trial; and then, if we perceived no
favourable movement in the ice, to retreat by Peel Strait, in
which case even we should have once more to get through
the pack which almost closed the northern entrance. To remain here at this season was out of the question. We were
hourly in danger of being beset in the pack, and if we could
not reach Bellot Strait on the following day, I decided to consider seriously our retreat to the northward.

Thus all my hopes were dashed to the ground; we were
helpless, and could not proceed by any human possibility—
no boat could get half a mile through this ice, nor could
anyone walk many yards on it. It was a dense mass of small
floes, intermingled here and there with large old floes. To
travel on the land was equally impossible, and especially
without the ship being fixed in some known and secure
position.

I now almost gave up all hope of our making the North-
West Passage this year; and, indeed, was more than ever of
the opinion that the only way to accomplish it would be to
proceed by way of Bellot Strait, there awaiting the moving of
the pack northward, and then pushing as fast as possible down
to Cape Victoria, for I thought that if the northern part of
Peel Strait was *entirely* free of ice, as we had found it, the pack
would be to the southward, as it was impossible that 120 miles
of ice could have dispersed, and it seemed more probable that it
swayed backwards and forwards, northward and southward in
the straits, until arrested by the frosts of September. We were

evidently on the northern edge of it, and as it probably impinged about the Tasmania group,[1] we could not hope for a
passage unless with a south or S.S.E. wind; and then we
should be, in our present position, carried back with it. Could
we but have reached Bellot Strait, I believe that this southerly
gale, which was evidently blowing with great force beyond
our visible horizon, would have eventually moved the ice up
northward, and have allowed us to proceed; but I could see
no chance of reaching the strait, for there was still one
mass of ice closely packed between us and the shore; neither
could I see any hope in the western horizon, for whenever
we attempted to go in that direction we were headed off
until we found ourselves steering north, and without any
indication of any lead of water along the shore of Prince of
Wales' Land.

We got several seals, and also shot a quantity of mallemokes for the dogs. Numbers of white whales were constantly
around the ship, but although we twice lowered a whale-boat,
with harpoon, gun, and line, we did not succeed in securing
one.

On visiting Roquette Island to-day, we discovered a
remarkable pool or small lake near the summit, completely
surrounded by mosses, and forming an entire circle. We also
saw many tracks of reindeer and several looms, thus proving
that the deer must cross to these islands on the ice in search
of food.

Seeing that the ship was being fast enclosed in the drifting
ice, I hastened down to the boat, and only arrived on board in
time to get the 'Pandora' clear of the island, as the ice-
floes were surrounding her; and we had to back in close to the
beach before we could get her head the right way. A gale

---

[1] The Tasmania group, on the west coast of Boothia, is at the south entrance of
Franklin Channel, which is the southern continuation of Peel Strait.

now commenced from the southward, with sleet, snow, and mist, and the northern edge of the pack began to break away and fly before the wind. There was only one course to pursue to prevent being beset, viz. to run before the gale and outstrip these sailing floes,[1] which had already preceded us on either hand.

[1] The whalers give the name of "sailing floes" to ice-floes drifting by the action of the wind.

BESET IN FRANKLIN CHANNEL.

CHAPTER XI.

A PERILOUS RACE WITH THE ICE.

WE drifted all night, with low sail, to the northward before the gale, in company with large and small floes and fields of ice, which gleamed through the darkness, and gave a weird appearance to the sea. We could not perceive anything at a distance of more than half a mile, and had constant alarms of a pack ahead, which, however, proved to be only streams of ice. By eight in the morning of the 2nd of September we had for half an hour a clear view, and I could see that we were close up to Barth Island, Roquette Islands being in the horizon, and surrounded by pack ice. By noon the wind came round to north, and blew a fresh gale with snow, and a new phase now came over the scene, for quantities of ice of a different description were coming from the northward, viz. fresh, unbroken fields of a year's growth, and with the smooth snow on the surface. I could not imagine where all this fresh ice came from, unless out of Browne's Bay;[1] it appeared to fill the straits northward of us, and we worked to windward the whole day, until up to Olrick Island, when we still saw more and more ice coming down, apparently filling the straits, leaving only a small space between the island and the shores of North Somerset; having reached this water, we commenced to dodge about for the night. I close-reefed the topsails, as they froze so fast after any rain or sleet, that we should have been in great trouble if we had had to shorten sail suddenly.

[1] A deep bay on the west side of Peel Strait.

The barometer had oscillated in a curious way during the last thirty-six hours, having fallen to 29·60, and rising at 8 P.M. to 29·85, with a dark gloomy sky, and a strong N.N.W. wind. On the 3rd of September we stood back towards the western land, having cleared the northern edge of the loose ice; but we soon met again a quantity of ice under the western shore, which quite frustrated my intention of landing and obtaining a view from the high cliffs. The wind came on at the same time from the southward, and began to blow in squalls, with snow and sleet. From the topmast head I could see nothing but the same dense pack of ice southward of us. There seemed no hope in that direction, and I reluctantly bore away to the northward before the gale.

Such, then, are the uncertainties and disappointments of Arctic navigation; for whilst on the previous Sunday we were running southward through these straits, which had never been previously navigated by any ship (unless Franklin had passed this way), with a clear sea, and with not a sign of ice, and every prospect of reaching King William's Land, and accomplishing the North-West Passage, we were, on the following day, arrested at the Roquette Islands by an impenetrable pack, and all our hopes frustrated. With the spring tides of the new moon I had hoped that the barrier might have given way, but no change had taken place, and I felt convinced that the fast ice extended right across from Kennedy Bay towards the Tasmania group. We had reached within 140 miles of Point Victory, and it was very provoking that we could not even proceed that distance, if only to return the same way.

On the 3rd we had the temperature about 27° to 28°, with barometer 29·60. We passed Howe Harbour at about 2 P.M. and continued northward under reefed sails until 8 P.M., when being close to the land southward of Wadworth Island, we tacked to the northward, and sounded in eighty fathoms, mud and sandy bottom.

I revolved in my mind the best course to pursue. To return southward again seemed hopeless, as we should only arrive at the edge of the pack which lay to the north of the fast ice in the straits, and which when we left it had accumulated up to Barth Island. We had already lost ten miles of ground. It was impossible to remain in the position we first reached at the Roquette Islands, for there was no harbour or bay in which we could anchor, and the ice was constantly coming down upon us from the north and compelling us to fleet up clear of it, in order to prevent being beset in a position in which we must necessarily have abandoned the ship the next spring, and have travelled to Fury Beach, Port Leopold, and possibly Beechey Island. This necessity would have made it impossible to explore King William Island by sledge parties. Moreover, even if this could have been done in the spring, it could not have resulted in finding any remains of the Franklin expedition beyond those obtained by M'Clintock and Hobson, who had made an exhaustive search, and whose footsteps we could merely have followed. Any additional search, to produce a useful result, must be made in summer when the snow is off the ground. To remain in the strait for the winter would certainly have involved the loss of the ship, as we could not have waited until the following August upon the chance of coming out, the northern part of Peel Strait being evidently only occasionally open. To proceed round by Regent Inlet to Bellot Strait appeared an alternative, but we had already seen at least ten miles of solid ice southward of Bellot Strait, right across Franklin Channel, with a bright ice sky, and no probability of getting southward this year by that route, in time to pass through to Behring's Strait.

We reluctantly beat to the northward all the forenoon against a northerly wind and in a close sea, and by noon we were again off Cape Granite, finding a wonderful change in the appearance of the land. When we passed down the strait a week before we could see scarcely a vestige of snow, except upon the higher lands in the interior; but now, even down to high-water mark, the land was so white as to appear like ice through the mist.

By 5 P.M. we began to see ice in the north-west, and so furling square sails, and steaming easily with fore-and-aft canvas, with the wind N.W. to W.N.W., we gradually drew up to Limestone Island; but a change now occurred; the wind began to blow in heavy gusts, with dense showers of snow, between which we could just catch a view of a solid pack to the westward, and of Limestone Island to the N.E. We passed close round Limestone Island, the cliffs towering over us through the snow, and the pack being scarcely half a mile to westward. The barometer fell rapidly to 29 50, and at the same time the temperature fell to 24° as we brought the pack to windward of us. I could just distinguish at intervals what appeared to be a sort of land water, about a mile wide, and I determined to run a race with the pack, and try to pass Cape Rennell [1] before it impinged completely on the land. This was our only chance of getting out of the strait, for had we hesitated, or stood back to the south-west, we should certainly have been shut in for the winter. We therefore pressed on into the gloom of the fast increasing darkness, and experienced a dreadful night, the wind increasing to a gale from the N.W. with dense sleet, hail, and snow showers in blinding drifts. To stop was impossible, for the pack, which was to windward, and seemed to be composed of enormous floes, unbroken for miles, was evidently coming in on the land, whilst on the other hand we constantly found streams of ice already jammed in the

---

[1] On the north coast of North Somerset. It was so named by Parry on the 29th of August, 1820, "after Major Rennell, a gentleman well known as the ablest geographer of the age."

shore, the points extending out almost to the main pack. Through this ice, or rather land water, of the width of one mile and a half, we threaded our way in the darkness, the white glare of the pack on the one hand, and the gleam of the snow-clad land on the other, being our only guides ; compass we had none, and once only during the night a solitary star shone out for about ten minutes, giving the helmsman a direction for steering.   We were on several occasions so close to the land that I thought we must run ashore, as we had really no guide during the snow squalls.   In the intervals we were frequently obliged to steer by the land astern, and it was somewhat ridiculous to see the helmsman facing aft at the wheel.   As the wind increased, and came over the pack, the temperature fell to 18° Fahr., and the spray froze over the ship.   By midnight our decks were full of snow, which whirled up in blinding drifts, from the eddy round the sails.

We could from time to time judge our position along the coast by the excellent descriptions by Sir James Ross and M'Clintock of their winter journey.   Thus, at 9 P.M., we passed a deep fissure or gorge, separating the limestone from the red sandstone, and which we had noticed when passing the previous week.   We continued on, the wind and snow increasing, and the pack evidently closing in, until 3 A.M., when we suddenly observed the ice to trend north and south right across our path.   I immediately hove-about, just clearing the solid floe ; at the same time a high, precipitous cliff showed out over us, presenting a most ghastly and horrible appearance, with a fringe of ice at the foot, and the horizontal strata appearing like huge bars of some gigantic iron cage, and perfectly black in contrast with the snowy face.   I could only see the summit, the strata, and the foot.   It was a skeleton of the land, and we appeared to be right within its grasp.   We saw this apparition for a few moments only ; running aloft, I saw from the topsail-yard that we were absolutely stopped and hemmed in a pool of

F

water, with no egress, and close under the cliffs, with the pack approaching. In a moment all was darkness again, and having got a pressure of steam, we forced the ship off the land, in the direction of the pack, for it certainly appeared as though we were to be driven on shore.

At 5.30 we had daylight, and I could just distinguish a break in the pack, leading towards the open water N.E. of us, but with a barrier of about 100 yards of ice stopping the way. There was no other chance, and to lose this would have been fatal; so, putting on all steam and sail, we ran at it and charged through, finding that it was not so solid as it at first appeared. We were again in the open sea, and, as I expected, our chief danger had ended at Cape Rennell. On getting through we appeared to lose all sight of ice ahead, and suddenly found ourselves in a rolling sea, covered, however, for at least four miles with young ice, or rather sludge, which acted like oil on the waters, and was so plastic as to take all the undulations of the sea.

Running on before the gale, we sighted Leopold Island in an interval of clear weather, but lost it again in a few minutes. At eleven we saw a heavy pack of ice to the south-east and east of us, so we hauled out to the northward to clear, and getting under two close-reefed topsails and fore-and-aft canvas, we banked the fires, to give the engineers a rest. The barometer now fell to 29·40, in the continued heavy snowdrift. We hove-to, only being able to see a few yards, and a high sea running, with a fresh gale N.W. Land appeared from Beechey Island, and twenty miles to the east on the north shore, and Leopold Island on the south, and we were evidently in a good position in the middle of the straits.

CHAPTER XII.

SECOND VISIT TO THE CARY ISLANDS.

On the 7th of September we got out of Lancaster Sound, and passed Cape Horsburgh, having for forty-eight hours been scudding under close-reefed topsails, in a heavy gale from the N.W., with a dense snowdrift, and the barometer down to 29·40. It was 22° Fahr., and bitterly cold, and the waves froze as they washed up our sides. We caught occasional glimpses of the north land, which guided us, for we could scarcely see at any time more than a mile from the ship, and we had neither sun, moon, stars, nor available compass, for the violent rolling of the ship caused our binnacle compasses, with their weak horizontal force, to spin round continually. Anxiously I watched our approach to Cape Bullen, for there, on the 22nd of August, we saw that the pack, which arrested us off Cape Warrender, extended quite across the straits. We then calculated that at least fifty miles east and west were entirely blocked, and it was only by working through narrow leads into the shore and the mouth of Admiralty Inlet that we succeeded in getting through. Now all was clear water, and by 9 P.M. on the 6th we had approached Cape Warrender, finding ourselves about half a mile from the glacier, a little to the west end of the Cape, and saw some heavy pieces of ice and many bergs, apparently aground, and experienced also a strong current running to the westward, causing the sea to break in a formidable manner, and in the gale that was blowing at the time the tops of this breaking sea frequently came over our quarters and taffrail.

Curiously enough, in scudding past Cape Bullen, we sud-

denly observed under the lee bow, or S.E. of us, what appeared
to be a pointed rock, about ten feet above the water, but which
proved to be only a piece of earth-stained ice.   This bears upon
the rocks which appear on the Admiralty Chart in Lancaster
Sound, on the authority of Captain Adams, which I do not in
the least believe to exist.

The state and appearance of our poor 'Pandora,' as we
emerged from Lancaster Sound was very extraordinary.   We
had been driving under close-reefed sails since escaping from
the pack off Cape Rennell, and the sea, which constantly
dashed against our sides, freezing as it rose, had covered our
ship on the port side with a solid mass of ice from the
doubling up to the rail, whilst the bows, from the figure-head
to the anchor, were all frozen into a solid mass, and looking
over the stern a fringe of enormous icicles hung down to the
water's level.   On deck we had a mixture of sludge, ice,
and snow, which required the whole attention of the watch
to clear off, and our poor dogs were in a most deplorable
condition.

Whilst at Ivigtut, on our outward passage, the sailors
bought a pig, which was petted to the last degree, and so
jealous were they of his rights that the dogs were driven in
all directions that poor Dennis, as they christened the pig,
might not be disturbed.   The dogs made several attempts to
attack this favoured animal, but a constant look-out—such
as one could never expect for ice, rock, or land from any
seaman on board—was kept, and the dogs were driven off at
the moment when victory seemed certain.   Pea-soup, broken
biscuits, and slops of all sorts were given to the dainty animal,
whereas if a dog attempted to ask for a share of the remains
of the sailors' dinners he was scouted with derision.   In fact,
the pig was the pet of the ship, and the only thing worth
navigating the Arctic Seas for.   Finding that he was
uncomfortable under the topgallant forecastle, and liable to be

disturbed by the chain running out when anchoring, or the water coming in at the hawse-pipe when at sea, a snug cask was found for him, and he was housed in with canvas and straw under the bows of the long boat. Never, I should think, had any other pig such comforts showered on him. But now came a change. Our decks became full of snow, and everything froze. It was necessary to clean away the ice and dirt from Mr. Pig's sty as well as from the other parts of the ship, and to do this involved an amount of scraping which was not agreeable to his former friends, and with the decision and readiness in meeting difficulties for which the seaman is so pre-eminent, the pig was condemned to death without remorse or apology In fact, from that moment he was a nuisance, and only fit to be killed and eaten: his throat was cut by his dearest friends, and he was eaten for dinner on the 7th of September, having died only at 10 A.M. Such are the caprices of our tars; but I must add that Mr. Pig's former owner sent an excellent joint to the ward-room, which was much appreciated.

It was now my intention to return to the Cary Islands, to ascertain if by chance the 'Alert' and 'Discovery' could possibly have called there after we left their letters on the 18th ultimo. I considered that after the 10th of this month the navigation of these seas would become a race against time, but I was not prepared for the violent N.N.W. gale which we had experienced during the last forty-eight hours. It had blown without ceasing, with a high breaking sea, and the spray drifting across the ship had frozen over all. We were one mass of ice. We had been standing to the N.E. and E.N.E. under close-reefed canvas, not having used our steam since passing Cape Rennell. The sea ran up in great heaps, and occasionally broke on board, and our prospect of getting northward appeared hopeless until this evening, when the gale moderated, and we got up steam and proceeded towards the

Cary Islands, which were about forty-five miles distant. At dusk we could just see Wolstenholme Island to the N.E., appearing like an elongated cone, and as a white shadow in the distance. We saw no signs of life, save a few malle-mokes, who shared the discomforts of the gale with us, and followed in our wake. The barometer, which had fallen to 29·40, was now rising, and the sea going down. I resolved to try to land on the island, and re-examine the cairn; but if this proved impracticable I determined to bear up for England, as nothing more could be done that season. The temperature averaged 23° to 18° Fahr. during the last forty-eight hours. It snowed nearly all night, but cleared over the eastern land about 6 A.M. I could distinguish Wolstenholme Island in the E.S.E., and the land about Cape Parry and Booth Sound in the N.E;

On the 10th of September all was dark to seaward. We were surrounded with icebergs of every conceivable size and shape, and the late gales appeared to have made great havoc amongst them, there being quantities of broken pieces in the water. Passing through one of these patches of broken ice, I took the opportunity to get a quantity on board, as we were quite out of fresh water, the last, which we pumped in from the floe, having proved to be brackish. Feeling confident of our position, and that we were close to the Cary Islands, although we could not see a mile to the westward, I hove-to until 9 A.M., when, the mist having lifted, I could see the S.E. Cary Island, distant about three miles, bearing N.W. Having determined to search all the islands of the group, so that there could be no chance of missing Captain Nares' record, if he had left one, I stood close alongside the S.E. island, and in passing saw a cairn. I did not at first attach much importance to this discovery, Captain Nares having said that his record would be on the N.W. island; but having so thoroughly searched the latter in August, I determined, if the weather permitted, to go through the entire group. Having rounded-to close under the northern side of the island, I dispatched a boat's crew, in charge of Lillingston, Beynen, and Toms, to examine the cairn. They landed with some difficulty, ascended through the deep snow to a height of 650 feet, and hastening on board, delivered to me the record case, containing letters, and an account of the proceedings of the 'Alert' and 'Discovery.' We were thus rewarded for all the hard work of the last few days, and for the risk in proceeding northward at this late season; and we had the satisfaction of bringing home news of the Government ships, which would be most welcome to the public and to the friends of all the members of the expedition.[1] Had we not returned this winter, or gone home with a report that nothing was known of the ships at these islands, considerable anxiety would probably have been felt. It was, however, by the merest chance that the cairn was seen, as I little expected to find anything on the S.E. island.

A notice was left in Captain Nares' cairn to the effect that we had removed his record and the letters for England, and explaining our second visit to the Cary Islands, and where he would find the letters which we deposited on the N.W. island in August.

The boat only just returned in time, for almost before she

[1] The Arctic Expedition sailed from Upernivik at 8 A.M. on the 22nd of July, 1875, and shaped a course due west, intending to make a dash through the middle pack instead of creeping round the land ice in Melville Bay. At 1 A.M. on the 23rd the pack edge was sighted, and the two vessels were at once pushed into it. The ice was very loose, not more than twelve inches thick, and with lanes of water in all directions. At 11 A.M. on Sunday, the 25th of July, the 'Alert' and 'Discovery' got clear of the pack and entered the "North Water" of Baffin's Bay, having been only thirty-four hours in the ice, and seventy hours in going from Upernivik to Cape York.

The 'Discovery' then went in shore to communicate with the natives at Cape York, and endeavour to engage a brother-in-law of Hans as second dog-driver. The 'Alert' proceeded to the Cary group, and reached the S.E. island at midnight on the 26th of July. Records and letters, as well as the depôt and a boat, were landed, and a cairn erected. The expedition then proceeded to Smith Sound, with the brightest prospect of an open sea, and of being able to reach a high northern latitude in the season of 1875.

was hoisted up, a blinding snow storm came up from the southward, during which we could not see a cable's length from the ship. Such are the dangers of cruising in these seas at this late season; it is absolutely unsafe to send a boat away unless the ship is securely anchored; the changes are so sudden and severe, that it is impossible to depend upon landing upon any exposed shore, or on again reaching the ship. I was only too thankful to see my boat's crew safely on board again on so awful a day.

CHAPTER XIII.

THE VOYAGE HOME.

On the 11th of September the sky cleared and the wind backed round to the N.W., and continued all day light with fine, clear weather. We were now steering towards the S.E., and by night saw Cape Dudley Digges about ten miles distant, the wind freshening to a gale, with a high following sea which froze as it lapped our sides.

Shortly after midnight on the 12th, we passed through a quantity of ice lying off Cape York, having previously gone through a complete chain of bergs, apparently aground, and reaching out from the land about the conical rock to twenty miles seaward in a S.W. direction. The storm was too heavy to think of sounding. I felt that we were going over a bank, but the size of the bergs was quite sufficient evidence that we had plenty of water, although the sea broke heavily over our quarters. It is curious how this ice appears to hang about Cape York, and I cannot help thinking that there must be an eddy current setting N.W. out of Melville Bay, constantly bringing up the ice which hangs about the glaciers and the land there, to the vicinity of Cape York; otherwise, in such a gale as we had experienced, it must soon have scattered to the S.E. By 4 A.M. it was almost daylight, and we were greatly relieved on finding that no ice was visible to the south or S.W., save a few large bergs. The gale diminished towards evening, and by six o'clock, after divine service, we got up steam and proceeded slowly through the night, with light variable winds. At noon this day our position by observation was 75° 2′ N., 65° 25′ W. Temperature 24° to 25° Fahrenheit.

The barometer rose and we had overcast weather with light east and S.E. winds. We had made since yesterday, about seventy-eight miles in a S.S.E. direction, and by noon could just distinguish the land about Wilcox Head and the Devil's Thumb. A high swell commenced from the southward, followed by a gale from the S.E. by E. to S.E., compelling us to heave-to under low sail. The night was intensely dark, sleet fell in showers, and everything seemed damp and miserable. We could only hope that we were well off the middle ice. The ship plunged bows under, but was quite buoyant and lively since having been lightened of her coals.

On the 14th and 15th we had a whole gale from S.E., with thick weather and constant sleet and snow, and a very high sea rolling up from south. We saw no ice save here and there a solitary berg, and lay-to under reefed topsails, occasionally to keep our position. On the 15th we saw an enormous berg, which, from its length, I at first mistook for Horse's Head. It was at least a mile long, and through the mist and gloom appeared still larger.

On the 16th the wind came round to the northward, and we progressed south, being at noon in lat. 72° 49′ N., long. 59° 4′ W., and next day sighted the land about the Svarte-Huk. About lat. 71° 31′, long. 57° 6′, we passed an immense number of large bergs, but we had not seen a piece of floe-ice since leaving Cape York, and I incline to the opinion that with a good ship, properly equipped and rigged to encounter bad weather, and the crew clothed for extreme variations of temperature, this would be the best month to make a passage northward through Melville Bay.

On the night of the 17th we had the first rain since entering Melville Bay on the 15th of August. The moon, which had shone so clearly for the last two nights, was quite obscured, and I consequently reduced sail, so as to have the ship under easy command in case of having to clear the icebergs or the land.

On the 19th we arrived off the harbour of Godhavn, having had variable strong winds since the 17th, and having run close along the west side of Disco with a N.E. gale until 8 P.M., when it fell calm. We came close past Fortune Bay and the off-lying islands and rocks, under steam; and when off the entrance to Godhavn we fired a gun, which was soon answered by a light on shore, and we anchored at 3 A.M. After passing Svarte-Huk, we saw and cleared a great many icebergs, which had possibly come out of Omenak Fiord. Several were also lying under the land of Disco, and in the entrance to Disco Fiord and Laxe Bay.

We sailed out of Godhavn on the 24th, having been at anchor four days, and not being able to leave earlier owing to a constant strong S.E. wind, with torrents of rain and snow all the time. On the 21st, Lillingston and Pirie went round to Disco Fiord in the steam cutter, returning all right, much to my relief, on the night of the 22nd, thoroughly drenched, and having had some difficulty in getting round, owing to the heavy sea outside. They had camped one night in the boat in the fiord, and brought back some ducks which they had shot. During our stay we filled up with water, and took in all our boats except the two whalers, and otherwise prepared for our homeward voyage. The crew had leave on shore every evening until 10 P.M., and the dance-house was open and the usual Eskimo ball kept up with great spirit until that hour.

The winds were principally from the north and east, occasionally freshening to a moderate gale, for the first five days of our homeward voyage. Our propeller was lifted, and we were fairly under canvas, having had our fires lighted up to the 25th instant, fifty-nine consecutive days, and still having forty-five tons of the best Welsh coal. We passed one or two icebergs, which appeared much broken by the sea; and although the nights had been intensely dark, we had had no occasion for any anxiety, as the seas had been almost free since leaving S.E. Bay and in the meridian of 55° which we had kept to. The barometer had been very low for the last twenty-four hours, 29·20 with overcast sky, and we had now baffling winds, with a tremendous and confused sea, principally from the S.E., and I supposed that a heavy gale was blowing round the land from that direction, especially as numbers of mallemokes were gathered around the ship. We were under close reefs, the ship rolling and pitching in such a manner as to make things thoroughly uncomfortable.

The high confused sea continued all night and throughout the next day, and I felt certain that a heavy gale had been blowing from the south-eastward, round the Cape, and that we were experiencing the eddy winds and back sea. Towards evening the wind became more steady from the N.N.W., but there was still the heavy pyramidal sea, which caused the ship to tumble in such a manner as to render it impossible to walk about. Hundreds of mallemokes flew around, and I observed a piece of drift pine about fifteen feet long and six in diameter. We lost two topgallant yards and a jib-boom, and were busy to-day making a new maintopsail yard. The barometer rose to 29·30, and the temperature to 42° Fahr.

On the 1st of October we had most brilliant displays of aurora, after which came frequent snow showers, ending in a brilliant morning. At noon we were to the southward of the Cape, and steering direct for the English Channel, Bishop's Light, Scilly, being 1651 miles distant, bearing S. 70° E.

We had fine weather until the 4th, with moderate breezes from the northward, but the magnificent auroras which every evening lighted up the heavens almost as brightly as the full moon, together with a rapidly falling barometer and a confused sea, all prepared us for the heavy gale which soon burst upon us, in lat. 57° 11′ N., long. 46° 3′ W. The wind

Ladies of Greenland.

commenced from about north, with heavy clouds full of rain, and then gradually backed to the N.N.W., when it blew with the utmost fury. I expected every minute that something would give out, or our canvas burst. A high breaking sea came up on the quarter, but by altering our course according to the change in the direction of the wind, we escaped being boarded by heavy water, although floods of spray came across us. The wind then settled down into a steady fresh gale from the W.N.W., and we scudded before it to the E.S.E., the barometer rising from 29·20 to 29·90, and the sea becoming more regular and true to the wind. We were in lat. 55° 54' N., long. 42° 44' W., at noon by observation, Scilly bearing S. 75° E. 1357 miles.

In the evening of the 5th, soon after eight o'clock, we had another brilliant display of aurora, which lighted up the sky and sea in a manner which I never before witnessed. It appeared first in the W.N.W., in luminous patches, at an elevation of 30 degrees, and quickly ascended towards the zenith, and almost immediately other corruscations shot up from the northward, extending across the zenith to S.S.W., and forming into vertical bands, having that peculiar serpentine motion so well known to Arctic voyagers. The reflection upon the crests of the seas was most beautiful, and as we scudded before the gale we could distinguish each break of the waves for miles astern of the ship. By nine o'clock the lights had quite disappeared, and high threatening clouds, arising in the westward, gave promise of a wild night. The barometer had risen all day, and it had been observed in running down Davis Straits that the mercury invariably fell with an approaching northward gale, being followed by a corresponding rise when the wind backed into the S.W. and southward.

A storm commenced on the evening of the 6th, so suddenly that we had barely time to reduce the canvas. It blew through the night, with torrents of rain and violent squalls, from

W.S.W. until morning, when it backed into the W.N.W., and increased until I thought that the close-reefed topsails under which we scudded must give out. We had frequent squalls of hail, and the sea increased to so awful a height that I feared we could not run any longer.

During the night of the 8th the sky presented the most terrific appearance; dense masses of clouds, apparently stationary, surrounded us like a wall, their upper edges illuminated with a brilliant aurora, making their centres and lower strata appear correspondingly black, and out of these black dense masses a sudden gleam of lightning would occasionally flash, like the flame from the muzzle of a gun, followed quickly by terrific blasts of wind and hail. The storm blew with hurricane force, still increasing, all the forenoon of the 9th; we battened everything down, and as it was not now possible to heave-to, I trusted to scudding before it, which we did all the forenoon, with heavy sea coming over both sides, and one over the stern, filling the deck fore and aft. I never saw so frightful a sea excepting in a typhoon or cyclone, and could not have believed that so violent a storm ever blew in extra-tropical latitudes. The barometer oscillated rapidly, sometimes rising above 30°, but never going below 29·20, and I was consequently little prepared for such a scene. However, we fortunately got through it, by extreme care in steering the ship, and without damage beyond the smashing of a boat. The storm abated about 4 P.M. on the 8th, the wind continuing through the night with occasional squalls from the westward, and the sea subsiding. The wind then backed into the S.W., blowing fresh, with rain, and a continuous gale from the westward for the next two days, before which we scudded under close reefs, and battened down. On the 11th the storm again increased, with violent squalls and tremendous sea, and we carried all sail possible, being frequently deluged with water. At noon we passed two barques, lying-to with nothing but lower maintopsail set. The barometer fell from 29·90 to 29·70, where it remained all day, and this was the only indication we had of the terrible gale we were experiencing. On the 13th we lost our jib-boom, and it was with some difficulty that we got the sail stowed, owing to the weight of water in it. The barometer at midnight was down to 28·90, and the wind suddenly backed into the westward until 3 A.M., when it as suddenly flew into the northward and N.N.E. to N.E., and blew with almost hurricane force.

We entered the Channel on the 14th, making all sail at daylight. In the afternoon a gale from the northward arose so suddenly that we had barely time to reduce to close reefs. We sent down topgallant yards and got the funnel up and screw down, and lighted the fires, but continued under canvas, and anchored at Spithead at daylight, on the 16th of October, 1875.

II.

THE SECOND VOYAGE OF THE 'PANDORA.'

1876.

CHAPTER I.

PREPARATIONS FOR THE VOYAGE.

THE 'Pandora' was laid up for the winter months of 1875–76 in Southampton Docks; her stores were landed, all perishable articles, including the salt provisions, were sold, and all her other outfit was sent to be overhauled and repaired. About twelve of the crew, mostly old followers of mine, were retained on board, and gave the ship a thorough cleansing throughout, besides refitting the gear, and doing such repairs as were required, and the ship was kept ready for immediate preparation for another voyage.

My intentions were to sail again on about the 1st of June, 1876, to make another attempt through Peel and Franklin Straits, and, by passing east of King William Island, to navigate the coast of North America to Behring's Straits. My experience of the ice block in Peel Strait last year caused me to think now much more seriously of the difficulty of passing through Franklin Straits, and grave doubts arose in my mind as to whether the passage in that direction is usually open, and the last season exceptional, or whether it was more frequently closed, and that it would be an exceptional year in which it would be found to be navigable. On the other hand, it is certain that Franklin's ships reached the N.W. point of King William Island in one summer from Beechey Island, but by which route, whether Peel Strait or M'Clintock Channel, it is not known. At any rate they got there, were beset on the 11th of September, 1846, and were finally abandoned nearly in the same position. Again, in the 'Fox,' when stopped at the western entrance of Bellot Strait, we had apparently only four miles of ice which barred our progress down Franklin Channel, and this ice seemed to be only lying in the form of *fast ice* attached to the islands outside Bellot Strait, leaving a navigable lane of water to the southward as far as visible from the high land. I had hoped last year by passing down Peel Strait, instead of Regent Inlet and Bellot Strait, to have been able to continue my course southward if the ice was in the same condition as we saw it from the 'Fox' in 1858. I had found, however, that while Peel Strait was entirely clear from Limestone Island to about five miles north of Cape Bird, the ice then extended right across the straits from east to west, forming an impregnable barrier as far as was visible from the highest land attainable (the top of La Roquette Island, about 280 feet), with a bright ice sky beyond. The barrier appeared to be composed of about five miles of loose floes, closely packed and driven down upon what seemed to be fast ice beyond, as if the straits had not broken up at all that year.

My impression at that time was, that owing to the extraordinary prevalence of strong N. and N.W. winds, the ice from the Polar pack had been driven through M'Clintock Channel in great quantity, and impinging on the coast of Boothia, had prevented Franklin Strait from opening during that season. Consequently I had determined to give it one more trial, and if I failed this year, to leave the grand feat of carrying a ship through from the Atlantic to the Pacific

Ocean in one season to some future navigator more fortunate than myself.

I intended to have commenced refitting the 'Pandora' soon after Christmas, so as to start fair with the new year, allowing plenty of time to make some alterations in the ship, and to select the crew. I determined to take the same complement of officers and men, and to provision the 'Pandora' in the same manner as last year, taking care to have everything necessary on board in the event of our being compelled to winter, and also in case we should have to abandon the ship and make a retreat over the ice or in boats. I was already beginning to make my preparations, when a communication from the Admiralty led to an interview with Mr. Ward Hunt and Sir Alexander Milne. This was followed by a letter from Mr. Vernon Lushington, dated 15th October, 1875, to the effect that their Lordships, having been informed by Captain Nares of his intention to send a travelling party from H.M.S. 'Discovery' to visit the entrance of Smith Sound in the spring of 1876, and perhaps also in the autumn of the same year, had under consideration the desirability of communicating during the summer of that year with Littleton Island or Cape Isabella. Believing that I was about to visit the Polar Regions, Mr. Lushington intimated that their Lordships would feel much obliged if I would assist them by making such communication, carrying despatches out and bringing home any notes or despatches which I might find at the above places. The letter added that should I receive this proposal favourably, they would feel themselves under a great obligation, and would consider it a public service; their Lordships also offered to pay any extra expenses caused by this deviation from my own route.

I was prepared for the receipt of this letter; and as the request was made upon public grounds, and couched in such

G 2

flattering terms, there seemed no alternative but to accept
their Lordships' proposal.

I therefore wrote to the Admiralty to say that I accepted
the responsibility in the light of a public duty, that the
'Pandora' would be prepared for sea with that object, and
that later I would apply to their Lordships for instructions.

My plans being changed, I had now to consider if it
was possible to combine the two objects, viz. to carry out my
own projects, and at the same time to do this work for the
country satisfactorily, both in one season. After much consideration, I arrived at the conclusion that it would be better
to leave my plans for Peel Strait for decision until I had first
done my best to carry out the views of the Admiralty, as it
was quite impossible to know in what state the ice might
be found, or how long we might be delayed in reaching Smith
Sound, even if we succeeded in arriving there at all. All
projects connected with Arctic navigation must necessarily be
very speculative, and it is out of all human foresight to anticipate events in those regions.

The 'Pandora' commenced refitting in March, and several
alterations and improvements were made. The combings of all
hatchways were raised; two deck-houses were built, one for the
use of the warrant officers amidships, and one aft to combine
our mess-room, the pantry, and my own cabin. By this arrangement we were able to use the old mess-room below for a store-
room and the two cabins opening out of it, one for a spirit-
room, and the other for clothing, tobacco, and chocolate. We
were thus enabled to stow 125 tons of coal under the deck
and in the bunkers. We also made our store-rooms much
more convenient and accessible. Many minor alterations were
made in the fittings on deck: the topsails were fitted with
Colling's and Pinkney's patent reefing and furling gear; and

all fore-and-aft sails were fitted with booms, excepting the two jibs. The steam cutter was stowed under the fore-boom on the top of the spare rudder, and the two cutters on the after-davits; the two whale-boats on the foremost davits, and the two dingies on the top of the midship house.

Provisions were stowed sufficient for thirty-three persons for eighteen months' full allowance, including all necessary clothing, travelling gear, whaling gear, and all the usual ice-implements.

The magazine was arranged in the stern, and we thus ensured our powder and ammunition being kept dry in the event of the ship springing a serious leak below.

The hydrographic and all scientific instruments were placed in the chart-room below, and the chronometers in a small recess outside Lieutenant Pirie's cabin. The library was placed in charge of the Doctor, and was arranged on shelves below, excepting such books as were in immediate use, and which were kept in the mess-room on deck. Our fresh water was all stowed in casks on deck, excepting a reserve of 200 gallons in a tank below.

The engineer's, boatswain's, carpenter's, and sailmaker's stores were all replenished, and everything having been put in thorough order, and all weights on board, the 'Pandora' was taken into dry dock to be examined and caulked where necessary. We found some slight damage to the false keel, arising from our having struck on a reef off the west coast of Greenland on our last voyage; but beyond this she had received no harm from her encounter with the ice and the violent storms we experienced.

The bottom was then partially caulked and coated with Peacock's paint from the top of the doubling to three feet under the water-line, and below that to the keel with coal-tar and naphtha.

*

My object in docking the ship with everything on board, including coals, was to ascertain if she was quite tight, as we had found a slight leak last year after the ship had been docked and had received her weights. This leakage was due to some bolt not being driven fairly when doubling the outer planking, and is a circumstance very likely to arise. I had the satisfaction to find that when loaded the 'Pandora' had no leakage. One other advantage in docking the ship at the last was that, as in the Southampton Water, the grass grows so quickly in the spring upon a ship's bottom, we left that port perfectly free of the weeds which so fouled the ship last year, and caused us so much loss of speed. In the meantime, the officers were selected, and the crew engaged; the chief difficulty being to choose those who appeared to be best fitted for the work before them; for as soon as it was known that the 'Pandora' was to try her fortune once more in the icy seas, I had a great many applications for appointments. I was only sorry that our limited space for accommodation and provisions, as well as the means at my command, compelled me to decline the services of many gallant young officers who so kindly offered to come with me.

The complement of the ship's company was thirty-three officers and crew, as follows :—

1. *ALLEN W. YOUNG, R.N.R. ..   *Captain.*
2. CHARLES R. ARBUTHNOT, R.N. ..   *Lieutenant.*
3. *GEORGE PIRIE, R.N. .. .. ..   *Navigating Sub-Lieut.*
4. *L. R. KOOLEMANS BEYNEN   *Lieut. Netherlands R.N.*
5. ALOIS RITTER VON BECKER   *Lieut. Austrian R.N.*
6. W. GRANT .. ..   *Photographer.*
7. *A. C. HORNER .. ..   *Surgeon and Naturalist.*
8. *Benjamin Ball .. ..   *First Engineer.*
9. *Archibald Porteous .. .. ..   *Second Engineer.*
10. *Henry Mitchell .. ..   *Gunner.*
11. William Taylor .. ..   *Boatswain.*

12.	*Robert James	.. ..	*Carpenter.*
13.	William Greenfield	.. .. ..	*Sailmaker.*
14.	*William Edwards	.. .. ..	*Ship's Steward.*
15.	*Charles Vine	.. ..	*Ward-room Steward.*
16.	*Thomas Florance	.. .. ..	*Captain of the Hold.*
17.	William Merrick	.. .. ..	*Ship's Cook.*
18.	*William Randerson	.. .. ..	*Quartermaster.*
19.	*Henry Andrews	.. .. ..	*Quartermaster.*
20.	William Berry	.. ..	*Quartermaster.*
21.	*Charles Tizzard	.. ..	*Boatswain's Mate.*
22.	*G. W. Thorne	.. ..	*Captain of the Maintop.*
23.	George Pearce	.. ..	*Captain of the Foretop.*
24.	*Allan Gillies	.. ..	*A.B.*
25.	William Owen	.. ..	*A.B.*
26.	William Ricketts	.. .. ..	*A.B.*
27.	William Battan	.. ..	*A.B.*
28.	P. de Gruchy	.. ..	*A.B.*
29.	F. Pressley	.. ..	*A.B.*
30.	George Smithers	.. .. ..	*A.B. and Captain's Coxswain.*
31.	Samuel Haines	.. ..	*Ordinary Seaman.*
32.	*Edwin Griffey	.. ..	*Ordinary Seaman and Stoker.*
33.	Henry Dennis	.. ..	*Ordinary Seaman and Stoker.*

Those whose names are marked with an asterisk (*) were in the 'Pandora' in her last voyage, and most of them had been retained on board all through the winter.

The above officers, petty officers, and crew signed the articles of the 'Pandora' on the 16th of May, 1876, agreeing to serve in the several capacities against their respective names on a voyage of search and discovery to the Arctic Seas, and until the ship was paid off at a final port of discharge in the United Kingdom.

Lieutenant Arbuthnot, who joined as first lieutenant and second in command, had applied to serve in the Government Arctic Expedition, and lately acted as gunnery officer in H.M.S. 'Invincible,' when he applied to go in the 'Pandora,' and I was very glad to secure the services of so experienced an officer.

Lieutenant Pirie had served as navigating lieutenant in the

'Pandora' in her last voyage, and again volunteered to accompany me. He had in the meantime been employed in the Hydrographic Department of the Admiralty, and I gladly availed myself of his services.

The Lords of the Admiralty granted to both of the above officers their sea-time and pay during their absence.

Lieutenant Koolemans Beynen, of the Royal Dutch Navy, was appointed by his Government to accompany the 'Pandora' on her last voyage in order to instruct himself in Arctic navigation, and was now a second time a volunteer by the desire of the Netherlands Government, and joined the 'Pandora' as an executive officer. Between the two voyages he edited a volume containing an account of the three voyages of his countryman, William Barents, to the Arctic Regions (1594–96), with a learned and exhaustive introduction, for the Hakluyt Society.

Lieutenant Alois Ritter von Becker, of the Austrian Royal Navy, was appointed by the Austro-Hungarian Government to accompany the 'Pandora' with a view to the study of ice navigation in the Northern Seas.

Dr. Arthur Horner served as surgeon and naturalist in the 'Pandora' last year, and again joined in the same capacity. He also had charge of the meteorological register.

Mr. Grant, who had been educated at Harrow and graduated at Oxford, volunteered as photographer, having made a special study of the art.

Mr. W. Taylor served as boatswain in the 'Assistance,' under the command of Sir Edward Belcher, and, notwithstanding his age, I was glad to engage so experienced and trustworthy an officer.

Thomas Florance, who had served in the 'North Star,' and under Sir Leopold M'Clintock, again joined in his capacity of last year as captain of the hold.

Many of the remainder of the petty officers and crew had served with me for some years in different ships, some of them in the 'Pandora' last year, and the others were all selected owing to superior characters they had received while serving in the Royal Navy or Merchant Service. When the crew was all complete, I felt that I could congratulate myself upon having a splendid ship's company.

CHAPTER II.

THE VOYAGE TO DISCO.

THE 'Pandora' being completed in her outfit, and ready for sea, left Southampton Docks on the 17th of May, 1876, and anchored in the river to receive her gunpowder, and to settle down the crew on board. On the 18th she proceeded to Cowes, and moored to the Royal Yacht buoy, when all the spare and old stores were landed, and all empty cases, portmanteaus, and casks were placed in my store there, as I intended on my return to dismantle and lay up at that port.

On the 22nd we proceeded to Portsmouth, and moored alongside the dockyard to take in the mails and despatches for the 'Alert' and 'Discovery,' and to await my final instructions from the Admiralty.

Whilst at Portsmouth, we had visits from many kind friends who came on board to wish us good-bye and all success, and I had the opportunity of obtaining the advice of my former commander, Sir Leopold M'Clintock, upon many points connected with our projected cruise. H.R.H. the Prince of Wales, with H.R.H. the Duke of Edinburgh, also honoured the 'Pandora' with a visit on the 23rd, and on that day I returned to London, to settle some private affairs, until the 27th, when we left Portsmouth for Cowes, the crews of Her Majesty's ships in harbour, as well as the 'Valorous' at Spithead, giving us a hearty cheer.

We again moored to the buoy in Cowes Roads, and, it being Saturday, some of the crew were given leave until Monday, in order that they might go home to arrange anything requisite before their final departure. Mr. Harper, my agent, met us at

Cowes, paid down all wages due to the men, and gave them allotment notes for half-pay to be allowed to their families, and, having settled all the ship's accounts with him, I returned to London until Wednesday, when, having all my affairs arranged, we left Cowes at 4 P.M., and ran out through the Needles under steam and all canvas. As we passed the Royal Yacht Squadron Castle, we were saluted by the battery. I had determined to be guided by the wind in the Channel whether to go east or west, and finding a light easterly breeze outside, as it was inside the Solent, we bore away for Plymouth to take in our last instalment of coals and to fill up water.

If the wind had been westerly, I should certainly have preferred to make the passage round by the North Sea and Scotland, as I am confident that at this season, and after my experience of last year, that is the better route in consequence of the prevalence of strong N.W. winds in the Atlantic between the parallels of 45° to 55° N. latitude, or, as the old seamen call them, the "roaring forties." But, with the prospect of a fair run out of the Channel, I determined again to try my luck in that direction, trusting either to get at once to the northward when clear of Ireland, or, if the winds should come in strong from the westward, to bolt through St. George's Channel, and out to the north of the Irish coast.

We had a pleasant run down Channel, and anchored under Drake's Island, in Plymouth Sound, at eleven o'clock on the 1st of June. In the evening we filled up with coals and water, taking about fifteen tons of coal in bags upon deck. We received the greatest attention from the authorities during our short stay. Admiral Sir Thomas Symonds and several officers, and other visitors came on board.

I had received a letter from the Admiralty giving me instructions as to their Lordships' desires with reference to my communicating with the entrance to Smith Sound in the event of Captain Nares having sent a travelling party there this spring for the purpose of leaving despatches or any information which he might deem of sufficient importance.

On arrival at Plymouth, I received a further letter from Admiral Robert Hall, saying that their Lordships desired to leave to my own judgment the steps that were most advisable for carrying out their general views.

It was a lovely evening when we slipped from the buoy, on the 2nd of June, and ran out of Plymouth Sound, receiving a hearty cheer from the training brig 'Liberty' and the yacht 'Speranza' as we passed. I felt some relief that we were at last fairly off, and putting all sail on the ship, stopped the engines, having a pleasant breeze from the N.W., and stood off on the starboard tack during the night.

Next day the wind came in strong from the W.S.W., and we commenced thrashing out of the Channel under canvas. By noon we were close under the Lizard, and made our number to Lloyd's station. This was altogether a disagreeable day, as it was our first breeze, with a nasty Channel sea and torrents of rain. Our screw was lifted and the funnel housed, and by evening we were under close reefs.

On the 4th of June the wind was S.W. to W.S.W. We stood all day to the N.W., made the Wolf Lighthouse at noon, and passed to the northward of the Scilly Islands, about four miles distance. At night we were again under close reefs, with a strong S.W. wind and a high confused swell. Divine service was performed in the evening.

On the 5th the wind was still S.W. to W., then N.N.W. We made all plain sail and pumped the water out of the boilers, by which we lightened the ship twelve tons. Since we had commenced knocking about in the sea, we found that we had a slight leak. I did not attach much importance to it, feeling sure that it was merely a repetition of what we found on our last voyage, and trusting either that the leak would take up or discontinue as the ship lightened.

On the 6th we were at noon in lat. 50° 23′ N., long. 8° 45′ W., and the wind continuing westerly I considered the advisability of bearing up for St. George's Channel; but as I did not like to give up any westing that we had gained, I stood on a wind to the northward, and saw the Fastnet Light. In the forenoon we had spoken a French fishing lugger from Boulogne, and the master came on board with about fifty fine mackerel and a ling, for which we gave him some salt beef. He reported that there were several of his fleet in the neighbourhood, and that they had had fair catches with their drift nets. He had now 15,000 mackerel, and intended in a few days to return home, and start again for the herring fishing in the north. We availed ourselves of this opportunity to send some letters. Our surgeon also prescribed for one of his crew, of which he had a complement of eighteen. His vessel was fitted with a small steam capstan for heaving in the nets. During the night we had the wind all round the compass, with a high confused sea and heavy rain. On the 9th we made some westing, and at noon were in lat. 50° 50′ N., long. 13° 46′ W., Cape Farewell being N. 62°, W. 1156 miles. We continued on the starboard tack all night, with a strong northerly wind, until eight on the morning of the 10th, when the wind backing into the westward, we tacked and stood away to the north; and I now determined, if we could weather the coast of Ireland, to get away to the northward as fast as possible, even at the sacrifice of our westing, and as the only means of securing a favourable passage across the Atlantic. Our experience of last year in July, and also that of the Polar ships in this month, proved that the best chance of avoiding the strong westerly and north-westerly winds and gales, and the continued north-westerly swells in making this passage, is to get as quickly as possible into a high northern latitude.

All the afternoon of the 13th we had evidence of an approaching gale. The wind gradually backed to the southward with a confused sea, torrents of rain, and the barometer rapidly falling from 29·82 at noon to 28·80 at 4 A.M. on the 14th. In the meantime the heavens had been constantly changing and the wind increasing in gusts. At midnight a bright "eye" was suddenly opened in the N.N.W., and then I knew that we should have a gale from that quarter.

Although fully prepared, I did not anticipate the violent storm which burst upon us. I had put the ship on the starboard tack to prevent our being taken aback, and during the early part of the day the weather cleared, the rain ceased, and the sun shone out brilliantly between the passing showers; but dense masses of *nimbi* hung round the horizon, with large patches of *cumuli* occasionally detached and flying across the zenith. The sea in the meantime began to roll in on pyramidal waves from the north, meeting the old westerly swell, and causing the 'Pandora' to tumble about in a most unpleasant manner. At eleven the gale arose in a sudden and heavy squall from the N.N.W., and we reduced canvas as fast as possible until we were under a balance-reefed main trysail and storm-reefed fore staysail. All other sails were stowed with extra care, and we at once commenced to batten hatchways and all openings, and secure everything. We were not a minute too soon, for the sea arose to such a height and commenced breaking so violently that we were flooded with spray and now and then the crest of a wave; but by lying-to and taking extreme care not to allow the ship to fall off, we rode tolerably comfortable, and escaped all heavy water and those formidable "breakers" which are so dangerous if they happen to tumble on board.

The wind blew as if nailed to the N.N.W. with almost

hurricane violence all the 14th and 15th and until 7 A.M. on the 16th, the squalls being so severe that it was wonderful how even our very small display of canvas withstood it. But we fortunately escaped without any damage whatever, excepting the loss of the head-boards on our starboard side. Our boats had been previously got in board and otherwise secured.

I was much interested in watching the fulmar petrels,[1] during the height of the storm, calmly resting on the waters in our wake on the windward quarter, and apparently quite at their ease and as keen as possible for anything they could pick up from the ship. I noticed that they always faced the wind, never allowing themselves to turn round for a moment, and just lifting themselves with their feet, and as it were with reefed wings, through or just over the crests of the sea.

By noon on the 16th we had driven back to lat. 57° 9′ N., long. 19° 48′ W., but the wind had moderated, the heavens had cleared, and we stood away again to the northward under all sail, and with varying fortunes in wind and weather until the 21st, when we were at noon in lat. 60° 57′ N., long. 31° 9′ W., Cape Farewell being 388 miles distant, bearing S. 83° W.

This was our highest latitude reached in the Atlantic. We were now nineteen days out from Plymouth, and I had every reason to be thankful that we had made so far a favourable passage, without a single hitch or mishap. Considering how very deeply our ship was laden, it was a matter of relief to me to find how well she rose to the seas. One thing I had always insisted on, and that was to keep the ship under as little canvas as possible in reason, as in my experience nearly all accidents with deep ships in the open ocean arise through carrying too much canvas, with the hope of making more progress, whereas the contrary is generally the case, for the ship becomes at once wild, and one plunge into a head sea, one

---

[1] See note, p. 6.

heavy lurch to leeward with a beam sea, or a broach-to with a following sea, may do more damage than all the gales with the ship well in hand.

I noticed in this passage an entire absence of the schools of porpoises which are generally met in this route, also of the finner whale (*Physalus antiquorum*) or rorqual,[1] which frequent the latitudes we had passed. We were usually accompanied by fulmar petrels (*Procellaria glacialis*[2]), Manx shearwater (*Puffinus anglorum*[3]), and a few skua gulls (*Stercorarius parasiticus*), and during bad weather by the charming little stormy petrel.

On the afternoon of the 21st the wind came from the northward, as I had expected, and soon freshened to a strong breeze, increasing to a heavy gale from the E.N.E., with very thick weather and constant rain. We ran under low canvas on a course to pass about seventy miles south of Farewell, and the sea rose to such a height that we were threatened with being pooped. By the night of the 24th I began to be very anxious about the chance of our falling in with drift ice. We watched the temperature of the water every two hours, and it gradually fell to 39°, when the most prudent thing to have done in such a gale and in such constant thick weather would have been to run off to the southward, but the sea was so heavy and breaking that it would have been impossible to bring it on our quarter, and therefore I had no alternative between running on before it or lying-to with our head to the southward. I chose the former, and nearly paid dearly for my determination, for about 2 A.M. of the 25th we fell in with small washed pieces of ice, and although I hauled out to the W.S.W. as much as I dared do for the sea, by five the ice became more frequent, and at six we came to a stream of very heavy and close pack lying across our path. It was too late to haul out now, and as we could not weather it, and there was nothing left but to take

---

[1] See p. 5 (note).   [2] See p. 6 (note).   [3] See p. 6 (note).

the most open-looking place and run through, the high sea
rendering it very difficult to distinguish the sea from the ice.
However, having selected one point where it appeared to be
most slack, I ran for it, and clewing up the close-reefed topsails, we passed through under bare poles excepting a fore
staysail, and by good steerage escaped, but not without some
violent blows. It was with a great sense of relief that on
trying the pumps we found that we had not received any injury,
and we again set the two close-reefed topsails, and scudded on,
keeping a course more to the south-westward, as the pack we
had passed through now defended us from the breaking sea.

This was a lesson to me, so often taught and again so often
on my part disregarded, never to trifle with this Cape Farewell
ice, and on no account to be induced by a fair wind and the
prospect of making progress, to run on in *thick weather* if
blowing hard and there is any swell on, and if within 100 miles
south of the land. I know too well the temptation to cut off a
bit of the journey, and after battling against constant head
gales in the Atlantic to take all advantage of a fair breeze to
run round into Davis Straits. But this temptation may
lead to a fatal error; and although one hopes that even if ice
should be met with, it may not be so close, or it may not be
so heavy, or we may forget for the moment past experience
in dealing with it, and only think of the escapes in other ice
navigation, yet I insist that it is the *most dangerous* position
that a ship can be placed in, for in off-lying streams it affords
no protection, and therefore no inducement to encounter it,
and in a heavy oceanic sea it resembles a mass of infuriated
rocks and islets, forming a lee shore of the worst description, if
you happen to run suddenly upon it. The only safe course to
pursue, in my opinion, formed after having been frequently in
encounters with the Cape Farewell drift ice, is, if running
before a gale from the eastward past the Cape, and the weather
is thick and the temperature of the sea surface goes below 42° or

43° Fahr., immediately to put the ship under as low canvas as
will keep her under command, and then dodge her with her
head to the southward until the weather clears up.   In doing
this a ship will not be altogether losing time, because the
current will drift her and carry her fast to the W.N.W.

On the 25th we continued scudding before the wind with
the two topsails close-reefed, the weather always thick, with
mist and rain and a heavy sea, passing icebergs and heavy
ground pieces.   Our position by dead reckoning was lat. 59° 4'
N., long. 47° 39' W.   We had not seen the sun since the
21st, and we could only hope that our calculation was correct,
and that we were now well round Farewell.[1]   At 10 P.M. we
suddenly came upon a barque, close-reefed and lying-to, with
her head to the southward, but passed her in the mist almost
immediately.   She seemed like a phantom ship peering out of
the gloom, and the quartermaster on watch was so taken by
surprise at the apparition that he ordered the helm " hard-a-
port," although we were well clear of her, and thus we lost an
opportunity of speaking her.   I think that she was one of the
ships trading to Ivigtut for cryolite, and was lying-to in the
storm awaiting clearer weather, and as a precaution against
the ice.

On the 26th we were still running before an E.S.E. wind,
no sun, and no relenting in the mist, fog, and rain.   On the
27th the wind hauled into the N.E. and the sky cleared, so
that we were able to get observations, the first for six days.
Our latitude proved to be 61° 56' N., longitude 54° 48' W., and
we found that we were but slightly out in our reckoning, only
about thirty miles to the N.W., and which was to be accounted
for by the current.

On the 28th we stood to the N.E. all day, and by noon
our latitude was 62° 29' N., longitude 55° 54' W. (N. 45° W.

---

[1] I ought to mention that the colour of the sea, in rounding Farewell during the last
three days, had quite changed from the oceanic blue to a muddy green.

45 miles).   At 6 P.M. I sent away a boat to an iceberg to get some fresh water from some débris of ice that surrounded it, and observing that the summit was covered with kittiwakes (*Rissa tridactyla*) roosting upon it, two guns were taken in the boat, but they only succeeded in bringing back three birds.

On the 29th we were still standing to N.E., with the wind fresh from N. by W.   At noon the latitude was 63° 20′ N., longitude 52° 55′ W. (N. 58° E. 96′).

As by our position we expected to pass over the bank marked here on the chart, I sounded at noon, and at 4 P.M., but found no bottom with 120 fathoms.   The weather had been thick all day, and so a good look-out was kept for the land, which we made at six o'clock, being one of the islands supposed to be off Buxa Fiord, but the weather was too thick and obscure to distinguish anything.   We then tacked to the westward, and as it was blowing hard from N. by W., with a nasty short sea, the 'Pandora' was put under snug canvas to await some more favourable change in the weather.

We passed many icebergs to-day lying about fifty miles off the land, and then suddenly came into a clear sea as we continued to the eastward, from which I suppose that they ground on the western end of the bank, and are unable consequently to approach the land beyond that limit.

On the 30th the wind was strong from the N.W. all night, with a high, hollow sea.   We stood off the land until 4 A.M., then in till noon, when we were in lat. 63° 57′ N., long. 52° 20′ W., having made since yesterday only N. 22° E. forty miles.   We tacked off and on all the afternoon, averaging about ten miles from the off-lying islands on the coast, in the neighbourhood of Godthaab.   This morning we sounded on the inside edge of the bank in forty-five fathoms, sand and shell bottom.   We detected that our progress to windward had been much assisted by the current, although from the appearance of the sea we could suppose a strong stream to the northward, causing the waves to curl and break in a manner otherwise unaccountable, and certainly not due to the force of the wind, which has not exceeded a double-reefed topsail breeze. We noticed this especially about the time when we sounded this morning, and there was a marked difference on getting into deeper water.

This evening the mist cleared off, and we had a pleasant view of the coast, with the gigantic mountains and icy valleys of the interior. I would have gone into Godthaab to avoid this persistent N.W. wind, only that I feared, as the settlement lies eighteen miles from the sea, it might involve my getting up steam when inside the islands, and our good Welsh coal is far too precious to expend without a better reason.

On the 2nd of July we had a gale from the south, lasting only about eight hours, and attended with snow and sleet. The wind backed at 4 A.M., the barometer falling slightly, and the temperature of the air going down to 32°, with dense weather. By 9 P.M. it cleared off, and came from the old quarter, N.N.W. This is the sixth day of baffling and head winds, and we have consequently made but poor progress. We stood in this morning to the coast by the entrance to the deep fiord, the northern entrance of which is bounded by old Sukkertoppen, and tacked about five miles off.

This delay was very tiresome and tedious, and quite unexpected. The weather, moreover, was unusually cold, and gave evidence of a backward season. We had divine service this evening, and the ship's company sang some hymns very creditably, Lieutenant Becker playing the accompaniment on the harmonium. I always find that seamen are most attentive at church, and the performance of divine service always seems to have the best possible effect upon them. It is the only occasion on which we all meet on the lower deck upon the same terms and with one holy object.

On coming upon deck after service the mountain peaks suddenly appeared above the fog, clear and brilliant, as if they were giving glory to the Almighty. The golden light of the sun was reflected from their summits into the heavens above, and they seemed almost to overhang the 'Pandora,' although distant at least ten miles.

We had an escort of kittiwakes constantly with us; they followed in hundreds, hovering over the stern, until suddenly attracted by something on the water they all darted off, but to return again almost immediately. It was also curious to observe the movements of the two or three skua gulls who seem to delight in chasing the kittiwakes.[1] They were always in company and always darting down suddenly on them, but without ever actually coming in contact. We had kittiwake stew for breakfast, which was excellent, and quite equal to the Bordeaux pigeon, if not better.

We had been beating, for the last two days, against a northerly wind, standing close into the coast of old Sukkertoppen, again near Ström Fiord, and again near Cape Burnit.[2] The wind persisted in the N.N.W., varying a point or two now and then, and we took every advantage to gain ground. One of my objects in keeping the coast close aboard was to ascertain if there was any current running to the northward here. We sounded at every opportunity, and the bottom which was brought up by the lead was carefully preserved.

[1] The kittiwake appears to find a small fish among the floating seaweed and immediately rises with it, and is then chased by the skua, who endeavours to make the weaker bird drop the food, upon which the skua at once pounces.

[2] There is reason to think that Burnit is a corruption, as in old charts it is Burnil; in which case it was no doubt named after Oliver Brunel, the earliest of Dutch navigators. In the Danish voyage to Greenland commanded by Cunningham Hall and Knight, in 1605, Oliver Brunel was one of the officers; and several names on this part of the Greenland coast refer to this expedition. There are the Knight Islands, Cunningham Fiord, after one of the commanders, and Cape Burnit (Brunel) after another. Lieutenant Koolemans Beynen has exhaustively discussed the history of Oliver Brunel in his introduction to the 'Barent's' voyages, and thinks that he also accompanied Knight on his ill-fated English voyage of 1606.

On this day we reached lat. 66° 56′ N., long. 54° 38′ W., and were off Holsteinborg. The wind, which came in from the west for a few hours this morning with rain, now returned to its old quarter, N. by W., with a brilliant clear sky. We looked forward to seeing the midnight sun on this night.

The sea was very smooth, although a smart breeze was blowing, and notwithstanding the vexation at this delay in our passage we enjoyed some rest after the incessant rolling in the Atlantic. All kinds of work had commenced, scientific and otherwise. The stoke-hole had been cleared of the coal bags and the boats got out and secured at the davits. The photographer had also begun some views. In the evening our little band of music might be heard on the lower deck, and everybody appeared in high spirits, excepting, I must own it, the Captain, to whose temper a persistent head wind, lasting already seven days, and spoiling an otherwise fair passage, had been rather trying.

CHAPTER III.

DISCO.

WE anchored in Godhavn at seven o'clock in the morning of the 7th of July   We had continued to beat to windward from the 4th, the wind remaining at N.N.W.   By 2 P.M. on the 6th we saw the high land of Disco, at eight we passed the Western Islands, and at eleven the Dog Islands.   We then got up steam for the first time since leaving the buoy in Plymouth Sound, and steamed into Godhavn.

On approaching the harbour this morning, there was not a sign of anyone moving : no boat came off, or kayak, and as it is so unusual at this season for the natives not to be out shooting or fishing in the early morning, I could not but think that there was some cause for this apparent indifference to our approach. This was, however, soon explained, for on opening the harbour we noticed that the large storehouse was unroofed and apparently burnt out; and as soon as we were anchored, Johan, the old schoolmaster, came off with a doleful story of how on the 17th of June, in boiling oil, the storehouse had taken fire, and the whole of the winter's production of oil and blubber—200 barrels—as well as all the stores belonging to the United States Polaris Expedition, had been totally destroyed. He related how he had been injured in the hand, as well as many other natives in their endeavours to arrest the flames and to save the property, and how almost everybody was sick at heart, and especially the Governor, who, he said, was very bad indeed, and unable to leave his house. There was gloom over the whole place, and the affair was evidently looked upon as a great catastrophe, such as we might consider the burning of half London.

My first business was to call on Mr. Edgar Fencker, the Governor, to inquire about his health, and I certainly found him in the most desponding state of mind. However, we did our best to cheer him and encourage him to take a happier view of things, and I am glad to say that by the time we left he had recovered his spirits. He requested me to survey the premises, and to give him a disinterested report with reference to the accident and the United States stores, which I gladly did for him, assisted by Lieutenant Arbuthnot.

On the 11th we had completed our refit, filled up water, made some alterations in the sails, re-stowed stores, prepared the after hold to receive coals, and put everything in order on board. The crew had leave every evening, and enjoyed themselves dancing with the natives. Pirie took magnetic observations with Jones's and Fox's instruments. Grant photographed everything of interest, and the Doctor was away botanizing each day. We also lost no opportunity of shooting ducks, and one night the officers all went off to Fortune Bay and brought back a good supply. We lived on eider ducks and salmon, which is here most delicious and delicate. It is a kind of salmon trout weighing about eight pounds, and when boiled is of a very pale colour. In fact we thoroughly enjoyed our stay in port, and all made great friends with the Greenlanders. The only drawback was caused by the quantities of the most venomous mosquitoes I ever saw, and they did their very best thoroughly to torment us. I never in any climate knew such a pest as we found these Greenland mosquitoes, for wherever we went, either on shore or in a boat, and even on board ship, they followed us persistently, and at whatever hour, night or day, it was always the same. I was this time more bitten than I ever was before. My head and hands were completely swollen, and one of my eyes shut up. Perhaps I suffered most from lying out shooting ducks on the ponds of the land.

Last Sunday we had divine service on the lower deck, and the crew sang several hymns very creditably, especially the hymn " For those at sea." We find the harmonium very much liked by all hands, and a great addition to our outfit.

I sent a kayaker round to Disco Fiord for Christian Anthone, who was with us in the ' Fox,' and on Sunday he arrived quite prepared to go in the ' Pandora,' and evidently supposed that was the object of my sending to him, so I agreed to ship him at 2l. per month as hunter and dog-driver, as well as inter- preter as far as he was able ; I gave him a new kayak, rifle, shot gun, and a kit of clothes and hunting gear; and he came on board quite happy. He left his wife and three children under the care of his brother, and she was to receive so much per month during his absence. He had been very poor, and seemed to have gradually gone down in the world, and was almost starving, having no kayak or rifle, and scarcely any clothes fit for work in bad weather. He looked, however, very well, and although it was nearly sixteen years since he left us in the ' Fox,' I could not say that age had told upon him. He was thirty-eight years of age. Anthone was at Disco Fiord last October, when Lillingston went there in the steam cutter, and he saw the boat, but having no kayak he could not cross the fiord, and thus was unable to come to see me, as I hoped he would do.

One day Pirie missed one of the small boxes containing a magnetic needle, after observing on shore, and on this being reported, the Governor sent for the head of the Greenlanders' Commune and informed him that it must be found and returned, and the whole settlement turned out to find it. It was produced later, apparently broken by the teeth of a dog, and was said to have been found among the dogs. However, we were glad to have it back, and looked upon the explanation as satisfactory.

I paid five Danish dollars for a kayaker to Disco Fiord and back, a distance of eighty miles, to tell Anthone to come. The charge for labour in watering ship was one shilling (English) and one glass of rum per man per day. I engaged a kayaker to come with me in the ship to Kudliset, eighty miles, to bring back letters, making a journey of 160 miles altogether, and an absence of four days at least, for ten Danish dollars and food whilst in the ship. The price of a new kayak and all implements is three pounds; dogs, four and five Danish dollars each; salmon, three for a shilling; ducks about twopence each.

I bought four fine dogs, intending to procure more at Ujaragsugssuk in the Waigat. At this season duck may be shot in any quantity by going to a point on the south-east side of the island and killing them as they pass in flights, having a kayaker with you to pick the birds up.

The best way to come-to, in Godhavn, is to anchor nearly in the middle of the harbour off the western houses of the settlement, and rather nearer to the western shore, in about nine fathoms, then run a warp to a ring in the rocks by the large storehouse, so as to prevent the ship going round and round her anchor, and having out about thirty fathoms of chain. I prefer this to mooring with two anchors, as then you have always one anchor clear for letting go if the wind should come in strong from any quarter.

CHAPTER IV.

KUDLISET AND UPERNIVIK.

WE steamed out of Godhavn at nine o'clock in the evening of the 11th of July, towards the Waigat, and arrived off Ujaragsugssuk at six o'clock on the evening of the 12th. We made a calm passage, with lovely weather.

I sent Arbuthnot on shore to request the Governor, Mr. Jansen, to accompany us to the coal mines with some natives to assist in working the coals, also to buy three dogs and harness. After three hours' delay, owing, I believe, to the priest and his wife having determined to take the opportunity of going with us as far as Kudliset, on their way to Narsak, and taking their time in packing their baggage and getting their umiak ready, and after blowing the steam whistle for some time, the Governor, the priest, and lady, with three daughters of the Governor and about twenty natives, came off, and we proceeded, anchoring at Kudliset at midnight in seven fathoms, about a small half mile from the beach.

We were coaling for two complete days and a half, and, having taken in fifty tons, we had altogether 175 tons of coal on board. The natives were of great assistance to us, but we had to feed them all the time, and moreover, more or less another party which came after us, and encamped in the neighbourhood for the purpose of bartering or selling some sealskins and other articles, and thus drawing considerably on our stores. They all seemed to think that a ship ought to provide provisions for all comers, and brought nothing whatever themselves, which is all very well when homeward bound; but bound as we were on an unknown and indefinite cruise, it was rather exacting, and it was very difficult to dispense the expected hospitality.

We had most lovely weather for our coaling, with a calm sea, so that our boats could land on the beach without any trouble whatever. We worked steadily from the time we anchored until we were full on deck and below, and I was out every night duck-shooting, at a point two miles northward of the mines, with more or less success. Our crew finished cleaning all the boats on shore, and washed all their clothes in a mountain stream which divides the cliffs here, and we sent our letters back to Godhavn by the postman whom we brought thence with his kayak. The Governor and family left us after dinner, all the workmen were paid, and we weighed anchor at 3 P.M., and steamed slowly out of the Waigat on the 15th.

On the 16th we were off Hare Island. A fair wind springing up at 8 A.M. we ceased steaming, but at night we were beating to windward, the wind having come to the northward. We were not yet round Svarte-Huk, which was about fifteen miles north of us. At six there was divine service on the lower deck.

In the Waigat the flood tide runs to the north-west, the ebb to the south-east, contrary to the streams of the tides outside the island, where the flood runs to the southward and ebb northward.

We have been in alternate calms and light southerly winds all the 17th, ending in a light north wind at night. Passing Svarte-Huk under all canvas, we then steamed for six hours, until 8 P.M., when we were off Kingulek[1] Island, and the wind freshening from the north, we stopped steaming and went on under canvas. I was anxious to save every pound of coal, and I did not intend to steam in the open sea unless it was calm. It was necessary to reserve all for Melville Bay, and the ice,

[1] *Kingulek* means scurvy grass (*Cochlearia Grœnlandica*).

and intricate channels beyond. It was most lovely weather, with a perfectly smooth sea and many magnificent icebergs. There was much snow on the high land, but at sea it was the brightest summer weather. We sat on deck and read, and skinned birds, and enjoyed the brilliant sunshine.

On the 18th we had light southerly winds freshening in the forenoon, and we ran to the northward under canvas towards Upernivik. We passed the rock which lies south-west from the Hope about nine miles. It is the most dangerous reef on this coast, as it lies quite in the track in coming from the south, and we were close to it before we discovered it just on our bow.

A fog came on as we approached the islands lying off Sanderson's Hope, and so I close-reefed topsails in order to lessen our speed; but, as it cleared off at noon, we made steam, and, passing between the two islands to the westward of the Hope, we arrived off Upernivik, and anchored in the outer roads in sixteen fathoms, midway between the two points next above the settlement. One day was occupied in exchanging visits with Governor Thÿgesen and Madame, who is the celebrated Sophia Tapita of Arctic history. We also bartered for skin clothing of all descriptions, and for eggs, of which the natives had a good store, although most of them were bad.

In the evening our men had a dance on shore, but as there were only five ladies, the ball was rather a failure, and a damper was thrown over it by one of the natives being seized with a fit. This was just after dancing a very pretty native dance, in which the opposite sexes stand in two rows. One couple, leading off down the middle, separate at the end, and an endeavour is made by the man to catch the woman, who dances round and in and out the others. When touched they fall in at the lower end of the two rows, and a fresh couple break off and begin from the top. This continues until a man has failed to catch his partner, when the dancing is reversed, and the woman now tries to catch her partner ; and so the dance goes on until she has also failed, when it is finished. It is altogether a very pretty and graceful dance.

The officers went off at 4 A.M. on the 19th in a whale-boat, rowed by natives, towards Sanderson's Hope to shoot looms at the rookery there, and returned at noon, having expended all their ammunition, and brought back 130 birds. We were all fully occupied on the 19th writing letters, photographing, and sketching, besides the visits to and fro to the Governor's house, where we met with the kindest reception. In the evening the Governor, with his wife Sophia, the priest, a Greenlander who had been resident two years in Copenhagen, and is the first ordained Eskimo, and a very intelligent agreeable person ; and Madame's servant Carlotta, a pretty Eskimo girl, came off to tea, bringing with them several presents, besides a cask of eggs. They all left at eight o'clock. We then weighed our anchor, finding that we had lost the stock, I suppose by striking on the hard rocky bottom of this anchorage, which is very bad, and also much exposed to westerly winds. In fact, a ship coming here should go at once into the Danish harbour on the north side of the settlement.

CHAPTER V.

MELVILLE BAY.

WE left Upernivik at 8 P.M. on the 19th, and stood out to the westward between Wedge Island and the Talbot Reef, when the densest fog came on that I think I ever experienced. We literally could not see fifty yards ahead, and were caught in a very difficult situation, being surrounded by islands of unknown size and position, besides icebergs. I put the ship under fore-and-aft canvas, going dead slow. At 1 A.M. of the 20th we just shaved a reef off the weather point of an island, and half an hour later we ran so close to another island ahead, that I had to go astern full speed and pay off before the wind with the sails. It was altogether a most anxious night, and I was glad when at 9 A.M. the fog gradually lifted as the north wind went down and we could see our way.

At noon on the 20th we were just south of Brown Island, in lat. 72° 35′ N., having only made twenty miles direct since the previous evening.

All the 20th and 21st there were light and variable winds, with dark weather. We passed the Duck Islands at noon of the 21st, and stood to the north until 3 P.M., amidst innumerable icebergs and many streams of floe-ice, which appeared very thin, and of one year's growth, and perhaps came from icebergs inshore. At 4 P.M. there was a dense fog, with wind fresh from N.N.W., and we were dodging until 9 P.M. under fore-and-aft sails, when we came to a very large floe, extending as far as visible east and west. We made fast to it with two anchors, to await a change in the weather, as I could not see 200 yards in any direction.

We were not destined to have much repose, for at midnight the floe broke away, and we were again adrift amongst the bergs, the fog continuing so dense that it was with the greatest difficulty we could clear them. We thus dodged principally to the N.E., tacking every ten minutes either for icebergs or streams of floe, until seven in the morning of the 22nd, when it cleared off, and the coast showed out in all its wild magnificence. We could see Sugar Loaf Hill bearing S.E., and round to the northward as far as Wilcox Head. Thousands of icebergs of every conceivable form and shape surrounded us, intermingled with drifting floes of ice, which almost blocked our way towards the north. We were about fifteen miles from Wilcox Head, bearing about E. by N., and the land ice seemed to be all broken up and intermingled with the bergs.

I never passed a more anxious week than that which ended on Saturday the 29th. It seemed to me like a year. On the 22nd we were sailing through wide lanes in the ice to the W.N.W., with a strong S.E. wind, having started off from near Wilcox Head towards Cape York. Our progress was rapid, the lanes opened as we proceeded, and, excepting an occasional *détour* to round an ice field, or a rush through a wall where the points were pressing together, or against an iceberg, we continued our course, and were in hopes of reaching Cape York and the North Water on the following day. But the weather became thick with mist and rain, and by midnight we could scarcely see to guide the ship. At 4 A.M. of Sunday the 23rd, we ran into a blind lead, and had to return out to the southeastward until 2 P.M., when, baffled in all directions, and the wind still blowing hard from the S.E., I made fast to a floe at the edge of what appeared to be an extensive open water to the south-west, intending as soon as we could in the least see our way out, to stand off in that direction, and dodge under canvas until the weather improved.

But on that night a complete storm arose from the S.S.E.,

with dense snow, limiting our range of vision to a few hundred yards. And what was my anxiety at 4 A.M. on Monday the 24th to find that we were completely shut in, in the drifting pack! One place seemed a little more open to the water in the S.W., and at this I immediately charged under steam and canvas. We succeeded in getting within half a mile of the water, and then the gale increased to a perfect hurricane from the S.E. The ice came driving along the outside edge of our coast line under which we were lying, and, accumulating as it passed, we had by evening at least four miles between us and the water; and the force of the gale began to make itself felt in the pack. The floes crushed together, and at 7 P.M. we had so severe a nip that the ship was hove over on her side, and the timbers began to crack in such a manner that we commenced blasting with gunpowder all round the 'Pandora' where the pressure seemed to be the greatest. However, all was of no avail, the floe still pressed sadly on our poor little ship, and two enormous icebergs came driving through it towards our position, causing more and more pressure.

At 8 P.M. things looked so serious that I ordered every preparation to be made to abandon the ship, the boats were all prepared for lowering at a minute's notice, provisions for one month stowed in them, the tents, sleeping, cooking, and travelling gear brought on deck, all ready to be thrown out on the ice; navigating instruments, fuel, spare clothing, medicine, &c., &c., with guns and ammunition, were stowed in the steam cutter, and in half an hour we were all ready to leave the 'Pandora' should she show any further signs of succumbing and sinking beneath the ice to the bottom of Melville Bay. How we were to escape afterwards was a question which passed constantly through my mind, for the ice was all broken in large hummocks in every direction, which would render it impossible to haul our boats over, and in which direction we should attempt to travel was so completely bewildering to think of, that I contented myself with taking only the necessary steps for our immediate safety should the ship go down.

It is at such moments as these that one requires all the self-possession at one's command, for the whole scene is too distracting to calmly contemplate any one point. The men are rushing about the deck, and on the floes with ice anchors, warps, and blasting gear. The coxswains are preparing and loading their different boats at the davits; the officers are each one preparing stores in his own department, and the whole tribe of dogs are fighting in a most frantic manner indiscriminately together, urged on by the excitement and bustle, and the prospect of some plunder. Wherever you move about the decks a battle is going on, accompanied by the most fearful noise, which of itself is enough to drive one mad; and had it not been that I looked upon them as so much live stock should we be turned out upon the floe, I really think that I should have ordered a general *battue* and a slaughter of these distracting animals.

Among the most painful episodes was the conduct of my faithful follower "Charles," who came every minute to me with something in his hand, or with an imploring inquiry as to whether he should save this or that article: clocks, photographic books, pairs of worked slippers, neckties, instruments, all my little valuables, which he knew I prized so much as the gift of some kind friend, and each time he looked more and more disappointed when I told him that we could think of saving nothing that would be practically useless on the ice, and that our whole attention must be given to provisions, warm clothing, and, beyond everything, to the arms and ammunition. Notwithstanding all my injunctions, Charles had, however, managed to conceal in the steam cutter every kind of thing—from a watch, boxes of cigars, eau de Cologne, two silver cups, to a cabin stove, and all the sea-boots and clothing, including a white shirt, wrapped carefully up in a worked Indian skin coat.

By 8 P.M. the nip eased off, and although the wind continued to blow in violent gusts from the southward, we lay tolerably quiet during the night.

On the 26th there were strong S.W. winds, and we were enveloped in mists, swarms of auks passing and repassing. In the intervals of clear weather we could see that the ice was accumulating outside, and that we were fast being driven into the middle of the pack.

On the 27th we were hopelessly beset; no water visible from the west, though a dark sky was seen from the S.W. to W., and a slight swell came in under the ice. We had no observations, but in the afternoon the weather cleared a little, and we could see land round Melville Bay for a moment only, and then all was mist and gloom again. The wind was still strong from the southward. I was in a frightful state of anxiety, which can only be understood by those who have been placed in a similar situation. We obtained an observation, in lat. 75° 43' and long. 62° 36', being our first glimpse of the sun from our position since the 22nd. Now there was no doubt about it, we were driven into the very heart of Melville Bay and could see no water. I incessantly studied Saunders's narrative of his besetment and drift in 1849 in the 'North Star,' and also that of our own in the 'Fox' in 1857, and I derived but little comfort from either, for Saunders was only released, after hairbreadth escapes, on the 25th of September to enter Wolstenholme Sound, while the 'Fox' never escaped at all, and drifted all the winter with the pack, until released the following spring in the southern part of Davis Strait. What was to be our fate? Were we to drift and drift with the pack through grounded icebergs and autumnal

*

storms, or were we destined by some intervention of Providence to be allowed to get free and continue the errand upon which we were employed?

The suspense on this day was awful. Deadly silence reigned around, broken only by the voices of the crew, who seemed quite happy at quiet prospects of "all night in," and were busy in washing clothes and various amusements. The officers were all out, walking or shooting, and I dwelling continually on this apparent arrest of our project. In the evening Cape Melville appeared close astern to the N.N.W., although it was actually distant twenty-five miles. Sleepless from anxiety, I remained up the entire night, listening with ear on the rail for the slightest sound or movement in the ice. Everybody was sound asleep. The death-like stillness so often described, but which can never be realized, was too awful. I felt that the 'Pandora' was in her icy tomb, and that escape was hopeless. Now and then I fancied I could detect a slight pulsation.

On the 28th Cape Melville, Cape Walker, and Peaked Hill, all showed out. We were in the heart of the bay, on the spot where 450-fathom soundings are marked on the chart. At last a murmur was heard on the ice, and it slackened slightly, and by 2 P.M. the huge bergs which surrounded us began to plough up the floes, causing a severe pressure on the ship. A lane opened, and we instantly pushed into it, and proceeded for about a mile towards water seen to the south-westward. At four the ice again closed up tight, and we could not proceed a yard, notwithstanding our frantic efforts and risk to our screw, besides heaving and warping, so we piped down to await events. In the evening thousands of auks flew past towards the water, which was now visible six miles from us in the W. and S.W. We shot many as they passed, besides several seals, only two of which we succeeded in landing, as they generally sink. Last night a bear came near the ship and was shot; three others were also seen prowling around, but did not come within our range.

At 10 P.M. the wind increased from the eastward, and by 4 A.M. of the 29th it was blowing a frightful storm from the S.E., with dense snow and sleet. We drove with the pack at a furious rate past some huge icebergs, and watched the floes as they piled up in front of them, calculating if we should clear them. To me this is the most awful feature of the pack. A berg is seen through the gloom; the bearing taken; questions asked how we are drifting; Is the berg aground? Shall we clear it? No! Then our destruction is at hand. Yes! Then we shall escape for the moment, unless the lateral pressure becomes too severe. We pass it, and can hear the roar of the ice smashing against its sides. The snow flies in dense eddies over its summit, like a cloud of steam; our floe is ground into the ship's side, and we are pressed into that on the opposite side, until the poor ship groans under the pressure; then the ice eases off, the ship comes upright, and we watch our approach towards the next mountain of ice which appears to lie in our path. It was altogether a fearful night, and glad I was when it passed away and left us in the morning of the 29th with a moderate breeze from the S.W., and the elements at rest. We saw the water nearer at hand, and made additional struggles to approach it; the ice alternately closed and eased, and we gained a few yards until 8 P.M., when a strong S.W. wind arose, and a distinct swell undulated through the pack. We could hear the breakers like the roar of surf upon a coast; the fog lifted, and we saw water, large water, open water, but two miles off, extending E.N.E. and W.S.W. as far as visible. All hands were called, we put on all steam, and after two hours of forcing inch by inch and yard by yard, we got into the sea, and were free. Cheers burst spontaneously from the

crew as we launched out into the ocean and made all sail to a
fair wind from the S.W.

Such was our escape.   To me the relief was so great that I
remained in the crow's-nest contemplating the dark blue sea,
looking inky black in comparison with our late ice world; and
as the 'Pandora' gave lurch after lurch, the boats and stores
and all on deck began to stray and roll about, and I felt that
once more I had the dancing waters under my feet.

CHAPTER VI.

A HURRICANE IN THE NORTH WATER.   CARY ISLANDS—
SUTHERLAND ISLAND.

WE were in the "North Water," and could bear away towards
Cape York, and thence onward in pursuance of our mission.
We were released upon the same day and nearly in the same
position as the ships of Sir Edward Belcher's squadron were in
1852, and we had the whole season before us.

On the 30th we were under all sail, with the engines
stopped, but with the same thick weather which had accompanied us since leaving Upernivik, we having had but one
clear day, and that for only a few hours since the 19th.   So far
we have come through storms and snow, and fog and ice.   We
steered a course as nearly as we could calculate to pass outside
Cape York.   At night it was blowing again hard from the S.E.
with snow and sleet.   We ran under close-reefed topsails until
4 A.M. of the 31st,[1] when the sky cleared and we found ourselves
off Cape Dudley Digges.   I then ran in close to the land,
passing just outside the ice which hung upon the shore, and
skirting this we were at 9 A.M. about a mile from Cape Athol.

We passed Wolstenholme Island in the forenoon and
steered for the Cary Islands, as I was anxious to visit the
depôt of the Polar ships in order to ascertain if it was intact
and to report thereon.   By noon it was blowing a gale from
the S.E., and we shortened sail to reefed storm trysail and
hove-to ; the mist so dense that we could not see half a mile
ahead.   Towards night the gale increased to a frightful storm
with a breaking sea, which washed in over all.   I ran to the

---

[1] The 'Alert' broke out of her winter quarters on July 31st.

N.E. to try to close the land for some shelter, but was headed off near Booth Sound by innumerable grounded bergs and wash pieces, and so I wore off at 9 A.M. with our head to the south-westward, and we lay-to through the night, the sea breaking constantly on board, and icebergs incessantly seen suddenly through the snow drift.

By 2 A.M. of the 1st of August it was blowing with such fury that the ship lay down to it, and the sea-drift blew straight over her. Our deck cargo had all fetched away, and began working in the lee scuppers. The boats at the davits were threatened, and our first whaler was smashed. The others were all secured or got on board, notwithstanding the risk attached to the manœuvre, and the men working up to their middles in water.

Such is a S.E. hurricane on this coast. No previous voyagers have experienced or recorded it, and I must confess that I was caught quite unprepared, and had little expected that within two days of our being apparently hopelessly beset in the pack, with quantities of all stores on deck in case of our having to abandon the ship, we should be laid down by a hurricane and forced to batten the ship down. As it was, and notwithstanding all the measures taken, we received a quantity of water below, and one of our best boats was almost destroyed.

The barometer gave us but slight warning, having fallen gradually to 29·38, which betokened nothing unusual in these latitudes. The only indication of the coming storm was the silent shroud-like clouds which capped the land all the previous forenoon.

By 6 A.M. of the 1st of August the gale moderated, but the sea continued to break in a most dangerous manner. We saw an island ahead which we made out to be the easternmost of the Cary group, and we got up steam and proceeded to it, soon making out the cairn which Captain Nares built last year, and which we visited in September last. All day we stood round and round the island, waiting for the sea to subside, and looking for a chance to land; and we descried the depôt of provisions and the boat on the southern point. But it was not till 4 P.M. that I could venture to send a boat away with Lieutenants Arbuthnot, Beynen, and Becker, who volunteered to go to examine the depôt.

By 8 P.M. the boat returned, and Arbuthnot reported that the island had apparently not been visited since the ' Pandora' was here on September 10, 1875, and that the depôt was in good order. Having deposited a record stating the object of our visit in the cairn at the summit, he returned as quickly as possible to the ship, according to my orders. Our photographer, Mr. Grant, also went on shore to take some views. Being rather short of water we delayed an hour, to load our boat with some pieces of ice recently detached from a grounded berg, and at nine I bore away for the north.

On the 2nd of August we ran all night before a pleasant and light southerly wind, passing west of Hakluyt Island,[1] and by 2 A.M. we were under all plain sail, with engines stopped. The west land was visible all the morning, but the shores of Prudhoe Land[2] were enveloped in mist, which cleared away towards midday, and gave us a splendid view of the stratified cliffs and glaciers, with the snow-capped mountains in the distance.

In the evening we rounded-to close to Sutherland Island,[3] sounding in twenty-five fathoms, sand and shells, about a quarter of a mile from the West Point, and I sent a party

---

[1] So named by Baffin. Its position was corrected by Inglefield in 1852. (See ' Summer Search,' p. 64.)

[2] Inglefield gave this name to the part of Greenland north of Whale Sound

[3] So named by Inglefield, in 1852, after Dr. Sutherland, the surgeon of the ' Isabella.'

on shore, consisting of Lieutenants Arbuthnot, Becker, and Beynen, to explore the island and to deposit a record of our proceedings.

Sutherland Island being one of the stations named by Captain Nares as a possible position for notices, I fully expected to find some despatch from him there, but after a thorough search of the island, which occupied four hours, our party were unable to find any indication of the Polar ships having touched there. They, however, found the remains of an old cairn, which had been either pulled down by the natives or the bears, and near it a broken earthenware blacking-bottle, half full of water, containing a fold of paper in a pulpy state, which proved to be a record, left by Captain Hartstene of the United States Navy, dated August 16, 1855, when in command of the steam brigs ' Arctic' and ' Release' he arrived here in search for traces of Dr. Kane.

The following is a copy of the record found on Sutherland Island, August 3, 1876 :—

" CAPE ALEXANDER, *August* 16, 1855.

" The U.S.S. Brig ' Arctic' separated from her consort the ' Release' on the morning of the 15th inst., off Wolstenholme Island, arrived here this day, and having made unsuccessful search for traces of Dr. Kane or Sir John Franklin and their associates, proceeded immediately on to Cape Hatherton for the same purpose.

(Signed)   " H. J. HARTSTENE,
Lieut. Commanding U.S. Arctic Expedition."

Written in pencil.

" Returned here from Cape Hatherton, Aug. 18, have received information from Esquimaux, Dr. Kane had lost his vessel and gone in his boats. I am going to Beechey Island.

" HARTSTENE.

" *Aug.* 19, '55.—I have returned from Cape Hatherton, and am on my way to rejoin you. If I miss you, remain off Cape Alexander till I return.

" HARTSTENE,
U.S. Brig ' Arctic.'"

Written in ink.

" U.S. BRIG 'ARCTIC,'
CAPE ALEXANDER,
Aug. 16, 1855.

" SIR,

"Finding no traces of the missing ones, I shall proceed immediately to Cape Hatherton in continuance of my search, where you will join. You will re-enter the record of our touching here together with another from yourself to the same effect.

" All your records to be within 12 feet north by compass of a cairn erected on the most conspicuous and accessible point.—Respectfully yours,

" H. J. HARTSTENE,
Lieut. Commanding Arctic Expedition.

"Lieut. CARL CHARLES C. SIMMS,
U.S. Barque ' Release.' "

Having erected a conspicuous cairn on the slope of the western point, our party deposited a record of our proceedings, and re-embarked, having had to pull through much loose ice both in going and returning. Mr. Grant took some photographs of the glacier on the main, from the summit of the island, and Lieutenant Becker shot a blue fox; a great many ducks and rotches were seen in and about the island, and some eggs, which, however, were already in a state of incubation.

The boat being hoisted up, I bore away round Cape Alexander, passing quite close to its foot, and soon opened Hartstene Bay, and observed Littleton Island,[1] towards which we steered, carefully examining all the indentations and bays as we passed, to look for a suitable harbour.

[1] Named by Inglefield, after a brother of Lord Hatherton.

CHAPTER VII.

LITTLETON ISLAND AND PANDORA HARBOUR.

WE arrived off Littleton Island at 2 A.M. on the 3rd of August, and found that the ice which we had observed all yesterday extending in a pack on our port hand from S.W. west to N.W. now trended round and touched upon the island, while some heavy pieces lay around the southern side.

On closing the island we observed a cairn on the summit nearer the eastern end, and so we pushed through the loose ice into the channel between the island and the main, which from aloft we could see to be open, and from the formation of the land to be deep. After passing the thickest of the ice I sent a boat ahead to sound, and we thus advanced slowly through this narrow passage without obtaining soundings with the hand lead, although at times we were almost alongside the rocks. Coming out on the N.E. side of the island I hauled round it towards M'Garry Island into a very narrow passage, and having sounded it and finding from three and a half to five fathoms (it was low water), I entered it and anchored, mooring the ship with warps to the ice foot with ice anchors.

I was in hopes that I should be able to remain in safety here for a sufficient time to search the island, but the wind now (6 A.M.) began to blow in gusts from the W.S.W. through the passage (the wind outside evidently blowing fresh from the S.S.W.), and heavy pieces of hummocky ice began to drive through and foul our warps continually.

Lieutenants Arbuthnot and Becker had started off in light costume to explore the island, and I had landed a quantity of provisions and sleeping gear in case of our being driven off. By seven o'clock, notwithstanding that we had taken our port bow hawser to the foremast head, the ice so continually fouled it and threatened to break us adrift that I determined at once to get out, and to dodge under the lee of the main island until we could pick up our absentees; so weighing the anchor, by careful manœuvring and guiding with the lines we managed to back out again stern first, after great difficulty, from the eddy gusts of wind and ice, and we lay-to off the N.E. corner of Littleton Island. I was so anxious about the party on shore that I could not rest for a moment, and when nine o'clock came and no signs of them, I felt very anxious for their safety. We had a loose driving pack on our north, the wind increasing, and the appearance of bad weather; and once separated from the island I knew not when we could again reach it. Fortunately the weather continued clear, and to my extreme relief at 9.30 our two absentees were observed coming over the hill towards our late temporary refuge. I immediately hoisted the ensign at the main, and sent on a boat which soon brought the party off, and also the provisions which we had left for them.

Arbuthnot reported that he had found three cairns, the larger one which we had seen on the summit, another nearer the centre, and the third on the slope of the western point. In the positions agreed with reference to this cairn he found a tin case containing the following record and despatch from Captain Nares, dated July 28th, 1875, and a closed letter addressed to C. Markham, which he had deposited there on his upward passage last summer :—

> "Arctic Expedition,
> H.M S. 'Alert' at Jansen Pt.,
> Hartstene Bay, 28th July, 1875.

"The 'Alert' and 'Discovery' arrived here this morning. As soon as I have examined the neighbourhood of 'Lifeboat Cove,' I shall cross to the west shore of the strait, and proceed northward on that side. There is now no ice in sight. Wind strong from north. Should the cairn not be visited by a sledge party from the expedition before June, 1876, our despatches will be found near a cairn on Cape Isabella. But if the strait is easily crossed, the sledge will visit this position.

"Should any letters for us be brought thus far, I request that they may be brought as far north as the vessel intends to come on the west side of the strait.

"If the vessel is not to enter the strait, then I request that our letters may be placed in my cairn on Cape Isabella.

"Should the weather not permit my visiting that position and establishing a cairn, I must ask the captain of the vessel to build one and deposit our letters 20 feet magnetic north of it, or in such other position as he may decide on, leaving due notice at the cairn.

"My intended stations on the west shore of the strait where cairns may be expected to be found, and which will be regularly visited as long as the expedition remains north of Smith Sound, are: Cape Isabella, Island off Cape Sabine, Dobbin Bay or Cape Leidy, Carl Ritter Bay, and Cape Bellot.

"All are well on board. A notice will be left on Sunrise Point — lat. 78° 20' N., long. 73° 15' W.

> (Signed)   "G. S. Nares,
> *Commanding Expedition.*"

From the contents of this despatch it was evident that no sledge party had visited Littleton Island this spring, and that the Polar ships had proceeded northward up the west side of Smith Sound. Our work then was completed so far as this side of the strait was concerned, excepting the desire expressed by the Admiralty that I should look for a suitable harbour for the relief ship next year. I therefore decided for the moment to return back towards Cape Alexander and endeavour to examine the bays and islands between it and Littleton Island. I considered, moreover, that if the supply ship was to be on this side of the straits, she should be near Littleton Island, or just southward of it, as the only position where she could be of any avail and free to enter and get out in the navigable season.

The wind had now (10 A.M.) freshened from the S.S.W.; the main pack lay off about four miles distant in the westward, and as far as visible in the S.W. round to north; but the loose ice had already driven north past Littleton Island, and I was enabled to steam round the western point, and in passing easily distinguished Captain Nares's cairn which is about 100 to 150 feet above the water, and which we did not see in coming from the South.

I now steamed back head to wind to Julia Glen Bay, and putting the ship under fore-and-aft canvas I continued dodging during the afternoon, as everybody was worn out with fatigue. The wind now blew in gusts over the land under the lee of which we lay.

This is a bay with a beautiful cascade pouring over the summit of the mountain, and falling with one drop of many hundred feet. The slopes of the hills are luxuriantly green, the verdure extending nearly to the very tops, and we were tacking in and out so close to the shore that we could see the white hares running about.

At 5 P.M. the wind moderating, though still blowing hard from the south, I stood in to examine "Foulke Harbour." I cannot recommend this small indentation in the coast, for it is really nothing more. We commenced sounding, and could get no bottom with the hand lead either in passing the three islands, Star, Knor, and Redcliff, or in entering the bight, and we proceeded until we were far too close to have thought of anchoring. In fact, it is nothing more than a little cove completely open to the west and south-west, and very unsafe, unless for a ship entering at the end of the navigable season and upon the point of being frozen in.

I then turned round into Foulke Fiord, sending a boat ahead to sound, and having also a lead line going in our fore chains. We found a piece of ice aground north of Star Island, apparently on a reef, and passing round this and getting into the centre of the entrance we obtained soundings varying from twenty fathoms to fifteen and ten, with uneven hard ground, and apparently forming a bar to the entrance. We soon passed over this, and when about the meridian of 73° by the chart we were again in deep water. We then steered towards the bay at the back of Port Foulke without obtaining soundings, except twenty fathoms when close in, and again no bottom. I then turned round towards the Huts of "Etah," which were visible on the beach, but deserted, and still finding deep water and the fast ice to extend from the southern point, enclosing the off-lying island to the Huts of Etah, I returned out of the fiord, and we dodged for the night off and on under canvas in Hartstene Bay with a fresh southerly wind.

I think that a harbour might perhaps be found round the back of the island and the southern point; but the fast ice prevented our going there to ascertain, and this ice was too rotten for us to hold on to.

This morning broke with a coming southerly gale, the ice began to set into Hartstene Bay in a most marvellous manner, and by 8 A.M. it had jammed in upon Littleton Island and Sunrise Point, filling the entrance to Foulke Fiord and gradually entering Port Foulke. To the west and south-west was a heavy pack, with occasional lanes of water; and several icebergs, which we had noticed off Sutherland Island on the evening of the 2nd, were now coming in fast towards Cape Kenrick. I got steam up, and pushed down to the Crystal Palace Glacier, but finding the ice still sweeping round Cape Alexander, I bore away for M'Cormick Bight, and placing the 'Pandora' as near the centre of the entrance as possible we sailed gradually in with a sounding boat ahead and leads in the chains.

We soon found regular soundings, beginning with 17,

then 15, 14, 12, and 10 fathoms, shoaling evenly to 8 and 7 as
we passed the narrowest part, and when in a fair berth formed
by the point extending from the southern shore we let go the
anchor in 6½ fathoms with a good bottom of mud, very black
and apparently very soft, as the lead sunk in to half its length.
I then veered to 30 fathoms of cable, and ran a warp to a
rock on the point, and we found ourselves to be in a fair
harbour, open only to four points of the compass. A reef,
which appeared at low water extending from the north shore
of the entrance, narrowed the exposed position by 15 degrees
less.

It was now high water (10.30) by the shore, and we rode
comfortably, the storm blowing in furious gusts *down* upon the
water, and I congratulated myself upon being safe at anchor.
Next day, if it was finer weather, I intended to have a rough
survey made of this harbour, which appeared to me to be the
only good one and fit for a relief ship to enter and remain at,
for it evidently has the advantage of opening early in the
season, has good holding ground, and is almost land-locked,
with room for several ships; and I doubt not that a ship properly moored might lie in safety here all the season, and until
she was fairly frozen in for the winter, if this was desired.

Notwithstanding the storm and the blinding snow, some of
our sportsmen immediately landed, and returned at 6 P.M. with
ten hares which they had shot on the slope of the southern
hills. As I wrote the gusts were coming over with such
strength as to heel the ship, but we held on with perfect confidence, and were content to see the ice driving past outside,
and some floes which in attempting to enter our refuge hung
upon grounded berg pieces on the reef off Reef Point, and
thus offered us still greater protection should the wind fly into
the westward.

On the 5th of August it continued to blow a heavy storm
throughout the night, but we lay quite comfortably in our

K

sheltered harbour. Three times in the night the officer of the watch called me to say that ice was driving into the harbour, but it proved to be merely isolated floes which passed round to leeward of the ship or grounded on the northern shore of the fiord.

The morning broke with a dark sky and falling snow, the gale still continuing from the southward, but evidently dying, and by 8 A.M. it was almost calm. After breakfast Pirie and Becker were away to survey the harbour, which I called "Pandora Harbour," as this was the first ship that ever anchored in it. At 10 A.M. I went ashore on the northern side, and ascended the hills up a steep face to a height of 700 feet, to have a look at the state of the ice in the straits. It was not a good view, as the air was misty in the westward; but I could see fifteen miles, and the ice appeared to be in considerable quantity in the straits, but broken up into streams. To the S.W. I thought that I saw an extensive pack, while to the northward the ice was closer, right into the entrance of Foulke Fiord and Harbour, filling Hartstene Bay, close up to Littleton Island, which it surrounded, and then stretched off to the W. and N.W. in a long stream; but as it was foggy in that direction I could not see if there was water beyond it. The Doctor and Anthone, the Eskimo, accompanied me, and we killed seven hares and about thirty rotches or little auks, which were assembled in thousands upon the precipitous rocks. Our sportsmen yesterday killed ten hares, besides some auks and ducks.

By noon to-day the weather was lovely, and so I prepared to start, and weighed at 5 P.M., having previously erected a cairn and placed a record on the point forming the southern projection of our harbour. It was full moon at 6.30 to 7 this morning, and it was high water at eleven o'clock, the rise and fall being about ten feet.

On weighing our anchor it was so buried in stiff mud that

we had great difficulty in breaking it out, and I was actually obliged to pawl the capstan, and go ahead with the steam before we could " water its hole."

Altogether this is a good harbour, and I hoped that I should be able to produce a rough plan of it from the observations of Pirie and Becker.

CHAPTER VIII.

CAPE ISABELLA.

I STOOD out to sea, steering a W.N.W. course, and as we opened the headland we found a strong northerly wind outside, with a dense fog coming on, so I put the ship under fore-and-aft canvas, and reached on through the gloom in hopes that we might not meet with the pack, and having steam and canvas in case of need. I was determined to make a great effort to reach Cape Isabella or Cape Sabine, as I believed that on that side would be found the despatches from the Polar ships.

Soon after our departure from M'Cormick Bight a thick fog came on, so dense that we could scarcely see a ship's length ahead; but as I had had a fair view of at least half the straits from the hills yesterday, and considering that the ice would only be found in loose streams, I pushed on under canvas. At midnight we passed through a stream of heavy ice without difficulty, and on the fog clearing off, at 2 A.M. of the 6th of August, we found ourselves about eight miles off Cape Isabella. Sailing close in under the land we anxiously looked for a cairn, and soon discovered one on the summit of the cape, when a landing party, commanded by Lieutenants Arbuthnot and Becker, immediately prepared to search for some record of the Polar ships, as I knew that this must be the 'Alert's' cairn, no other ship having ever visited the coast. The wind was blowing hard from the northward, but the weather was clear, so no time was to be lost. The 'Pandora' was laid to windward of the point, and the boat shot off among the loose drifting pieces of ice which hung

THE CAIRN, CAPE ISABELLA.

under the shore. It was a moment of extreme anxiety to me, and I would have delayed their departure, but here a fog might arrive or a southerly gale come on, and we should lose the opportunity, perhaps not to occur again.

The 'Pandora' was kept close to the shore; but we soon lost sight of our party among the cliffs and ravines on shore. Hour after hour elapsed before I could distinguish with a telescope two figures at the cairn, and it was not till 4 P.M. that the boat returned on board, having been absent ten hours.

In the meantime the wind had freshened to a gale, and it was with difficulty that we kept our position with the ship, and when the ebb-tide began to make, about 11 A.M., masses of heavy ground ice came streaming round the point to the southward.

My anxiety had been increased when at 1 P.M. the boat having been reported as coming off, she passed behind an iceberg aground close in, and was seen no more. We were all immediately on the alert, and after some time our boat was seen hauled up on the shore, about half a mile to the southward; but we could not see the people, who were afterwards descried running over a hill-side, and then I feared that the boat had been crushed, and that the crew were on the hill to attract our attention. A boat and rescue party was immediately ordered away, and the ship pushed in towards the land; but the tide ran with such velocity as to endanger her being thrown on the rocks. Presently I saw Arbuthnot calmly examining another cairn, and the recall was immediately hoisted; but we saw that they were rolling up our cask of letters towards the cairn, and then I knew that all was right.

Lieutenants Arbuthnot and Becker reached the cairn on the summit at 11 A.M.,[1] having been two hours in securing the

---

[1] This cairn was erected by Captain Markham on the 29th of July, 1875. The 'Alert' had left the Cary Islands, after depositing the depôt, on the 26th, and Captains Nares and Markham visited Littleton Island on the 28th.

＊

boat on the ice foot. They found Captain Nares's record of
July 29th, 1875, and also a smaller cairn on the hill lower
down, and bearing magnetic west from the summit, near
which a depôt of provisions was placed. Arbuthnot removed
our cask of letters for the Polar ships to this spot from the
place where he had first landed, and hence the explanation of
our alarm at the sudden disappearance of the boat.

The following is a copy of the record found on August 6th,
1876, at Cape Isabella :—

"ARCTIC EXPEDITION,
H.M.S. 'ALERT,' AT CAPE ISABELLA,
29th July, 1875.

"'Alert and 'Discovery' erected this cairn 29th July, 1875. Should
the strait be impassable for a sledge, the despatches from the expedition will
be deposited in a cask, on the lower point magnetic west of this position, each
spring of our stay north of Smith Sound.

"Anyone having despatches or letters for the expedition is requested to
deposit them in the casks, unless he is coming farther north. In that case, a
cairn will probably be found at Cape Sabine, Dobbin Bay, Carl Ritter Bay,
and Port Bellot.

"All well on board. No ice in sight. Should the strait be passable, the
despatches will be taken to Littleton Island.

(Signed)   " G. S. NARES,
Commanding Expedition."

A record from the 'Pandora' was left here, giving par-
ticulars of our proceedings up to this time, and also stating
that having visited the cairn at the summit of the Cape, and
carefully examined the point mentioned in Captain Nares's
record, and finding no signs of any sledge party having visited
Cape Isabella from the Polar ships, our cask of letters had
been placed at the point named, and close to Captain Nares's
depôt of provisions; and that the bulk of the letters, with the
Admiralty despatches, would be carried farther north if
possible; if this were not possible, they would probably be
placed on Littleton Island.

I did not think I could ever imagine a more desolate coast
than this appeared to be. The land seemed to be covered with

everlasting snow, and might be said to be one vast glacier, with merely the capes protruding towards the sea. It was horrible to look at, and frightful to contemplate the results of disaster to a ship's crew thrown upon it.

Towards evening the gale died away, our absentees were safely on board, the boat hoisted up, and we stood away to the N.E. under steam and fore-and-aft canvas, with a strong but steady breeze from the north. We did not see any ice to the northward, save a few heavy ground pieces and isolated floes; but there was an ominous yellowish-white tinge in the sky in the N. and N.E. I hoped, however, that we should be able to reach Cape Sabine at least.

Looking into Baird Inlet, it appeared about half full of ice, the precipitous cliffs seeming to afford no anchorage. It looked like a vast cavern in the land, black and frowning, with a glacier at the bottom, and forming the two points of entrance. I then went below for a little reflection. I had been on deck for twenty-nine hours, ten of which were passed in utmost anxiety, watching our boats on shore; and now that the excitement was over, I felt that I had time to consider my plans. We were proceeding towards Cape Sabine, the ship was quiet, and, in fact, everybody excepting the watch, sound asleep. As we drew up towards Cape Patterson, I began to think that it was necessary to examine the empty cask at Cape Isabella, referred to in Captain Nares's record, for letters and despatches. Arbuthnot, thinking it contained provisions, had not disturbed it.

At this time ice was reported ahead, and, in going to the crow's-nest, I found that the pack lay from the shore about Leconte Island, out to the eastward as far as I could see. This decided me to return to Cape Isabella in order to examine the cask, and so we immediately ran back before the wind, which increased to a gale from the north before we reached the cape at 3 A.M. A boat was prepared, but the storm came so

*

strong, and the ice came driving by so rapidly, that I did not send the boat away, for even though steaming full speed we could not hold our position against the wind and tide.

We were now helpless, and had to put the ship off to the eastward through the streams of ice. Day after day I continued to struggle against wind, and ice, and fogs to regain the cape and effect a landing. On more than one occasion we were within two miles of it, but always the same driving masses, through which no boat could survive for an instant, nor could she have regained the ship if once within them. I tried all hazards and forced the ship through such ice as I had never before seen. We had laid to the floe in thick weather at the risk of being beset, and at last, on the 9th of August, I was fairly driven over to the east side of the strait by an enormous pack, which extended right across from Gale Point to Littleton Island, and coming rapidly down before the northern gale I made all speed, anchoring at 3 P.M. in Pandora Harbour.

Could that cask contain Captain Nares's despatches? There was no record to be found near it. The cases were marked "New Zealand" meat, H.M.S. 'Discovery,' but the cask was not examined for any mark. I had certainly given positive orders that no provisions were to be disturbed on any account, and thus our difficulty. Arbuthnot arrived at the conclusion that the cask contained provisions only, because it was placed with the meat tins. He had therefore reported to me that he could find nothing beyond a depôt of provisions.

But, on reconsidering the whole question, I came to the conclusion that I must make another attempt to reach Cape Isabella before going north. For the whole results of our voyage depended upon getting news which would inform us whether a sledge party had actually been to Cape Isabella.

CHAPTER IX.

ATTEMPTS TO REACH CAPE ISABELLA.

NEXT day, if it was fine, I intended to go to Lifeboat Cove, and try to get a view of the ice from Littleton Island. The weather was very boisterous outside, and quite fine in Pandora Harbour; our sportsmen were all out; a reindeer had been seen, and I went away bagging ducks as a distraction. The 'Pandora' looked very tired after our late battering, and several severe scores in her bows and sides showed what a severe battle she had endured during the last week; indeed, I had given her one or two blows which almost sent my heart up into my mouth. The ice we encountered seemed to be oceanic, together with heavy hummocky ice formed in the bays, tide creeks, and nips on the beach, and so unyielding that with the slightest speed in the ship it brought her up all standing, and threatened to smash in her bows. Fortunately we had sustained no material damage, nor had we injured our screw or rudder. We were all well, and ready for another struggle as soon as we had had time to rest. But a more tired-out crew I think I never saw, although they were in the highest spirits, and keen for the work before them.

I had given up all idea of my own project to try for the North-West Passage by Peel Straits. I felt that I must stop here until the end of the navigable season, if not during the winter, and everything must be sacrificed to the one object of obtaining some information of the Polar ships. We were bound to cruise these straits to the last with that view, or upon the chance of a boat party coming down.

On the 10th of August we were fast to the edge of the pack, sixteen miles off the cape, and preparations were made for sending a sledge party, but we had to return to Pandora Harbour, a strong southerly wind having come on with thick weather. While at anchor our sportsmen killed about sixty hares and some ducks, so that we had plenty of fresh food. I erected a cairn north of the harbour, placing a record magnetic north stating our movements. On the 13th we went out again, and got about ten miles from the cape. We had a boat and sledge party again prepared, but the driving ice, the northerly gale blowing, and the dreadful weather, quite precluded all idea of sending .a party away from the ship. Thus day after day passed away, and we were helpless. We could not get into Cape Isabella, although our repeated attempts sometimes gave hope. All the 13th and 14th we lay-to in a north gale with the ice driving in great streams to the southward. I had hoped that the pack would be driven away, but on its clearing at noon, the same unbroken curve from about Cape Paget in the west round to Cairn Point in the east lay before us. We could not get north, nor could we regain Cape Isabella ; but we had to struggle in the middle of the straits with ice, fogs, and winds. I did not like returning to harbour, as there was so much off-lying ice that it might set in and make us prisoners for some time, so we cruised continually across the straits from side to side, through the pack, awaiting events, but unable to do anything beyond keeping the ship under control, and avoiding the heavy masses of the heaviest ice I ever saw.

On the 16th of August there were strong northerly winds, with the main pack coming down to the southward, and extending from as far as possible in the S.S.W., round towards Cairn Point. No water was seen in any direction in that quarter. On the previous evening I steered up between the pack and Littleton Island, and tried to get to the northward, as the ice seemed to ease off the land. By 4 A.M. we reached a position N.W. of Cape Inglefield in lat. 78° 45', and about seven miles off the land, Cape Sabine bearing W.N.W.; but here the ice brought us up and extended in a curve into the land about three miles N.E. of us. It was composed of the heaviest pieces, forty to fifty feet thick, lying in streams, and then the unbroken floes and hummocks as far as visible from the crow's-nest, stretching from shore to shore.

I came to the conclusion that these straits had not broken up this year owing to the prevalence of southerly winds all the spring and summer, and that the ice we saw was the solid winter pack moved down some distance by the north winds of the last eight days. It seemed an exceptional season, for all to the northward was one solid barrier. We could see the land up to Cape Hawke this morning. The land on the east side was impossible to distinguish from the chart, as the capes and points do not bear the test of the sextant in attempting to verify them.

We tried a series of soundings with Negretti's and also Casella's thermometers, and when one mile west of Littleton Island we could get no bottom with 150 fathoms. The temperature of the sea surface and air was 28°; while at 25 fathoms and 100 fathoms it was 33° Fahr., thus showing a current of warmer water running in on this side of the straits. Moreover, we found a constant difference of about three degrees in the temperature of the sea between the east and west side of the straits, and with our other experiences of a northerly set in the east side, I have arrived at the conclusion that the permanent current sets northward on the east side and southward on the west at Cape Isabella. Where the line of division lies I am not able to say, but I should give it, from watching carefully the ice movements, at about ten to fourteen miles west of Littleton Island.

Finding that it was impossible to get northward by the east side, I ran back towards Littleton Island in order to get a larger space to lay-to in, and thus avoid the use of steam, as we have been so constantly of late burning coals to clear the ice; and at 4 P.M., seeing that the ice slackened in the direction of Cape Isabella, I once more ran before the strong N.N.E. wind under canvas in that direction. It was only, however, to be again baffled. The S.W. pack had eased off, leaving the space of one mile of broken and loose ice to within seven miles of the cape beyond, which was a jumble of hummocks and a pack of broken heavy pieces, through which the ship could not force, and over which one could not travel, or move a boat; so I came out again into clearer water to escape being beset. The heavy fog to the southward, and clouds arising in that direction, indicated the approach of a southerly wind.

On the night of the 16th, when three miles N.W. of Littleton Island, we saw three walrus on a small piece of ice, curled up; and going away in the first whale-boat, I succeeded in securing one weighing about 18 cwt., a female with only one tusk, and measuring thirteen feet from snout to flipper. We hove her in with the capstan and fish tackle, and took a photograph of her before cutting her up. At twelve o'clock, three miles west of Cairn Point, four more walrus were seen on the ice. We lowered two boats and captured them all after a most exciting chase. Pulling up to them we wounded two with our rifles, and our Eskimo, Anthone, put his lance into another, which was soon despatched on its again rising; another came up to the jolly boat, and Becker hacked at its head with an axe until he lost the axe overboard, and finally killed it with his rifle. In the meantime we in the whaler had two wounded, and coming up occasionally; but one was shot through the head, and the other was fired into with the harpoon gun and secured. In the middle of the scrimmage the old boatswain, who was left in charge of the ship, thinking that we were in difficulties, steamed up full speed right on to us, thus increasing the confusion, and nearly smashing the ship's bows in the solid pack, off which we were. We got all four walrus safely on board, and with the one which we captured earlier in the evening we had about two-and-a-half to three tons of meat and oil. At 4 A.M. another group was seen, but our fiendish dogs were fighting as usual, and disturbed them, and we did not succeed in getting near enough to kill them with the boats, which we lowered.

In the afternoon I stood back towards Cape Isabella, but could not get within eight miles of the land, the intervening space being filled with the same broken-up pack of heavy hummocky pieces.

In the evening at 5 P.M. whilst in the loose S.W. pack, the wind suddenly changed to the southward, and I stood on under fore-and-aft sails, and back to the western land, where we lay-to until 8 A.M.

When I stood back again towards Cape Isabella, on the 17th of August, the wind which had blown freshly throughout last night, did not appear to have made much change in the ice. We entered the pack at about thirteen miles from the cape, and when about seven miles off we could still see the same accumulation of hummocks, bergs, and smashed-up ice, extending to about six miles off the cape. Seeing that it was impossible to land there, I again stood out of the pack into the clear water in the eastward.

We had been sounding to-day, and after several attempts we got bottom with 650 fathoms, about half-way across the straits, between Littleton Island and Cape Isabella. The bottom was a soft and greenish mud, and a beautiful starfish was brought up from it clinging to the line. This specimen of the deep-sea fauna measured three feet when the tentacles were

outstretched, with five rays, from which double branches sprung
of a yellowish-brown colour, very sluggish, but quite alive
when brought on deck, and answering to the description of the
Asterophyton linckii, figured in Professor Wyville Thomson's
'Depths of the Sea.'[1] The temperature of the sea surface was
34° Fahr., while Casella's thermometer registered 29° when
brought up with the sounding machine.

I became more and more anxious about our position. We
could not proceed north, for the main pack still extended from
as far as possible in the south-west, round in an unbroken curve
to Cairn Point. Ever since August the 3rd, when we arrived
at Littleton Island, we had been crossing and recrossing the
straits, or attempting to get northward. It was the most
fatiguing work I ever had, this battling with the elements of
storm, ice, and currents. I had already anchored three times,
but only for a few hours at a time, as I was too anxious to keep
the ship outside and under command, so as to avail myself of
every opportunity offered by a change in the ice, which seemed
destined not to occur. I resolved, however, to struggle on, in
the hope of yet regaining Cape Isabella, and clearing up the
mystery about the despatches, and of proceeding northward, if
possible. One thing certainly occurred to me, that although it
was my duty to remain in these straits as long as I could—and
I intended doing so even at the risk of wintering there—yet
from the present appearance of the ice, which completely filled
the sea from shore to shore in the northward, it was evident
that no boat expedition nor the Polar ships themselves could
possibly come southward unless some great revolution took
place before the end of the month. We already had signs of
an approach of the autumn : the birds were beginning to fly
southward, as the young birds were strong enough, and even

---

[1] P. 19.—In 1819, on the 1st of September, Sir John Ross brought up one of these
beautiful creatures on the lead line, at a depth of 800 fathoms, in 73° 37′ N. He called
it "Caput Medusæ." The 'Valorous' obtained them off Hare Island.

on our last visit to Pandora Harbour the rookery of auks was already nearly deserted.

On August the 20th we were still cruising in the entrance to Smith Sound. We had since the 17th been again twice across towards Cape Isabella, but had not succeeded in getting within seven miles. This was most harassing work. We were continually entering the pack, and sometimes saw a promising lead, towards the land, then a change of tide would close it all up, or a thick fog or change of wind, and we were obliged to back out again, and each time at extreme risk of being beset in the S.W. pack, and carried away with it. This pack still persistently stretched from S.S W. as far as could be seen, close to the land and round in a curve to Cape Hatherton, where it rested on the shore, moving slightly north or south according to the wind and tide, but it never left either shore, nor was there ever any break through it. It was in just the same state as Dr. Kane showed it on the chart of his voyage in 1853–54, during each month of August. It was composed of the heaviest ice, 40, 50, or 60 feet thick, some of the pieces being an accumulation of blocks heaped upon each other by severe pressure, and it was impossible to strike it with the ship without danger of starting something. On one or two occasions, when unable to avoid it, we struck it as if upon a rock. I had a theory that this ice was the forerunner of the great pack clearing out of Kane Basin, and that these heavy pieces at the edge were the floes found along shore, near the tide-creeks and amongst the grounded bergs.

Oh! Isabella, you have given us one opportunity, shall we ever have another? It would be unlike your sex; but ought not our perseverance for three long weeks and our constancy to touch your heart and cause you to relent?

In the afternoon of August 19th it was calm and fine. We lay three miles west of Littleton Island. I took the steam cutter with the dingy, and asking all the officers to accompany me, I went into Lifeboat Cove to visit the scene of the Polaris encampment and wreck.[1] Passing M'Garry Island we saw two walruses on the ice, but as we had no harpoon, and I was anxious not to delay, we pushed on, and were surprised to find enormous flights of ducks passing round and round the island. The sea was also literally covered with rotches, the young birds assembling in thousands, apparently receiving their education in swimming and diving preparatory to their departure on their long flight southbards. This was very encouraging, as for the last few days we had seen nothing of them at sea, and I had almost concluded that the migration of the birds had already taken place.

We soon made out the point on which the 'Polaris' was run on shore, and on landing we found the site of the house. But it was entirely destroyed, not a vestige remaining save a few broken pieces of wood. All around, among the rocks and on the beach, we found various relics, such as lamps, old boots, and clothing, parts of machinery, torn paper, copper utensils, and almost every twenty yards, caches formed of stones, some of which still contained walrus beef, while the walrus heads were strewn plentifully about in all directions, but all having the tusks sawn off close to the skull.

Although I had reason to suppose that the 'Alert' touched here, I made a careful examination for anything like the books, instruments, or a record, but I only succeeded in finding in one place (in which I consequently gather that the instruments were originally stowed) the copper box of a seven-inch compass, and some parts of a telescope with a long tube, which might

---

[1] The 'Polaris' was grounded at Littleton Island on the 16th of October, 1872. The day before nineteen persons had been left on the ice; and only fourteen men remained with the 'Polaris,' namely, Captain Budington, Dr. Bessels, Mr. Chester, Mr. Morton, Bryan, Schumann, Odell, Coffin, Booth, Campbell, Mauch, Hayes, Siemens, and Hobby. It was found impossible to remain in the ship, so they built a wooden house on shore. During the winter they had much intercourse with the Eskimos at Etah. The party left Polaris House in boats on June 2, 1873, and, as is well known, was picked up by the 'Ravenscraig' whaler in Melville Bay on the 22nd, lat. 75° 38' N., long. 65° 35' W. They left many books and instruments behind, in caches.

have been part of an astronomical telescope. We found also four gun-barrels cut in half, as if to make pistols, many Eskimo arrows and spears, and one lamp with Sidney Budington scratched on it. But the whole place appeared to have been subjected to the most wanton destruction, and the storms of the winter had scattered the remains.

Whilst we were still on shore a gale suddenly sprung up from the southward. Our ship was five miles off, and much drift ice, or rather heavy shore ice, passing with the current, so we made all haste to the boat, pushed off, and arrived on board the 'Pandora,' thoroughly drenched with the heavy sea which arose immediately with the wind. We had some difficulty in getting the boat up, but eventually all was safe, and we stood towards the pack under fore-and-aft canvas. We saw no traces of any recent visit of natives, and the caches of walrus meat were in a putrid state. I had hoped to have found the Eskimos, but I supposed that they had not yet come northward.[1]

[1] I was more fixed in my opinion than ever (after having watched the ice continually night and day since the 3rd instant, and having crossed and recrossed the straits at the edge of the pack, and through any navigable ice, sometimes being ten miles within the pack), that a relief ship ought to be here continuously during the stay of the Polar ships northward, for I could not see how Captain Nares was to get his ships down at all, if such a pack as we found should be here again next season. It appeared to me that if he was well-upon the west side, and could not get back with his ships this season, he would travel next spring over the ice, dragging the boats with him, and striking across from Cape Sabine to Littleton Island. The channel had certainly not been open, for even boat navigation, up to this time, since our arrival; and it was here, at Littleton Island, that he would require the boats, should the relief ship fail to arrive.

CHAPTER X.

SECOND VISIT TO CAPE ISABELLA.

FROM the evening of the 19th until the morning of the 23rd[1] we had a gale from the southward, with snow, sleet, and rain. We hung on outside until the 22nd, when it came on to blow with such fury that I went into Pandora Harbour for the night. We found some loose ice, but it was mostly aground round the inner shore, and did not incommode us. We took advantage of this opportunity to fill up eight casks of water from off one of these pieces. During the night of the 22nd the squalls came down over the high land into the harbour with such fury as to drive the spray over the ship, and the men watering on the ice had to be careful that they were not blown off. We held on securely with only thirty fathoms of chain, the anchor sinking right over in the stiff blue mud. It moderated on the 23rd, and at 8 A.M. I left the harbour to view the effects of the storm upon the pack outside; but there was the same thick weather as had prevailed for the last five days, which prevented our seeing any distance in the westward. For a few moments only it partially cleared, and I could then see from the crow's-nest that an enormous pack had driven up from the S.W., past Cape Isabella, and from our position six miles west in the straits we could see no water in the direction of the cape. The northern pack had driven right up to the N. and N.E., and between it and the S.W. pack there was a crack in the W.N.W. to N.W., the north pack

---

[1] On the 20th the 'Alert' and 'Discovery' crossed Lady Franklin Strait on their way home, and rounded Cape Lieber. On the 23rd they anchored in a small bay near Cape Fraser.

CAPE ISABELLA.

apparently then extending from Cairn Point round to Leconte Island, towards which there was also a darker appearance in the sky I pushed for this crack, but a thick mist coming on, and the floes again closing together, I was obliged to stop.

All the afternoon the weather was still thick, with light northerly wind and rain. There appeared no hope of reaching Cape Isabella or of getting northward, and I seriously considered what was the best thing to be done with our remaining despatches and letters. As we were every day in danger of being beset in the pack in our attempts to get westward, I resolved to land them at Littleton Island, as the best course for all concerned. So at 10 P.M. I went away with a party and deposited them on a low point N.N.E., magnetic, from Captain Nares's cairn on the west point of the island. I placed them (three casks and four cases) about sixty feet above the sea, in a crevice in the rocks, where they are hidden from the natives in travelling round the coast on the ice, marking their position by a small cairn. A notice and a letter to Captain Nares were deposited near his cairn (magnetic north). I re-embarked at 11.30, the rain falling in torrents, with a fresh north wind, dark and thick weather, and very cold and miserable, for I felt that this was one step towards the completion of our voyage. We had cruised here in gales, fog, and drift ice ever since the 3rd of August.

The season was fast slipping away, and we seemed only to lose ground, for the north wind brought down the N.E. pack, and a south wind brought up the S.W. pack. Every other day it blew a gale, and in the intervals we had fog. We had, however, much to be thankful for, as we were all well, the ship undamaged, excepting a bent blade of the propeller, and everybody in good spirits.

We noticed an extraordinary rise in the barometer previous and up to the height of the storm from the southward, and it afterwards fell when the wind came round to the north. The air felt softer, and our sails remained soaking wet, contrary to my expectations, that on the change of wind they would be frozen up. Could it have been that there was much water beyond the pack to the northward? The sky was dark, overcast, and misty, and the heavy mist clouds over the Greenland coast appeared to work up from the southward. We had not seen the western coast except for a few minutes for five days. The ice was so heavy that the gales appeared to have no effect in smashing it, and after each storm we found the same solid line. During the late gale we had a considerable swell from the south in the open space between the ice and the land, but, beyond the slight movement of the bergs and a broken edge in some places of a few yards only, the ice did not seem to yield to the sea as it does in other waters. The young birds were assembling in flocks, and flying off to the southward. On our visit to Pandora Harbour on the 22nd, the rookery of little auks was already deserted. We still found a permanent current of about two miles an hour running northward by Littleton Island, checked only for a few hours by the ebb tide.

At 3 P.M. we noticed that the pack slacked towards the W.N.W., and the sky looked darker in the direction of Baird Inlet than we had yet seen it. I felt that now or never would be our chance to get over to Cape Isabella, so, putting on plenty of steam, we pushed boldly into the pack, and although we could scarcely see our way, we got in by 8.30 into a sort of land water by Leconte Island. The fog lifted for a moment, and we could just see the top of the island close to us, with the gleam of the glacier south of it; but the air became so dense again that we were obliged to stop altogether. We had the pack on one side and the land on the other, and I could see nothing else to do but to wait until we could see something more. A drizzling rain falling at the same time, and the wind increasing from the southward, made our position anything but pleasant; and, to add to my anxiety, I found that the ship was being continually whirled round by the current, although in what direction we were being borne I could not guess.

At 10.30 the air partially cleared, so that we could detect the high peaks over Cape Isabella. I immediately went full speed towards the cape against the wind, which was now strong from the south, with continuous sleet and rain. We passed Baird Inlet at 11.30, finding still a land water with loose streams and floes, and by 12.15 we were under the very rocks of Cape Isabella. Not a moment was to be lost. We had been struggling for three weeks through and through the pack in all weathers, and at last we had regained the cape. It was clear down to the sea, a number of grounded pieces only resting on the rocks, but continuous streams were coming round before the wind and flood tide. We pushed the ship within half a cable's length of the rocks, and hurried off the landing party in the dingy, as that boat was considered more convenient for hauling over the ice, if her retreat should be cut off. Three waterproof bags for the letters were placed in her, besides coopers' tools; and anxiously we watched the party land and ascend the hill. They lost not a moment; in twenty minutes we could see them at the cairn, and a few minutes afterwards descending the rocks; but, alas! with the bags empty hanging over a pickaxe on Arbuthnot's shoulders. Even then I hoped that his haversack at least might contain some despatch; but, on their arrival on board, Arbuthnot reported that on opening the cask (the cask for which we had laboured night and day, and had at last reached), it was EMPTY![1]

Arbuthnot also reported that he had examined the cases,

---

[1] August 25th. The two Arctic ships were on this day off Louis Napoleon Head, only 85 miles from Cape Isabella. They rounded Louis Napoleon Head and Cape Hilgard on the 27th.

*

and found them to contain preserved meat. They were carefully closed again, as was the empty cask, and the hammer and driver which were also found under the cask, were left in the same position. I could only conjecture that Captain Nares had landed this cask on his way up Smith Sound, to save its weight to the contemplated sledge party from the ships to Cape Isabella in the spring, and in order that a water-tight receptacle might be at hand for his despatches, and also for any that might be brought out for the expedition.

When Arbuthnot landed here on the 7th, and deposited *our* cask of letters for the Polar ships, he also placed a record of our proceedings in the lower cairn close by. He had now added to the record that further letters and despatches were left on Littleton Island.[1]

---

[1] When the 'Alert' and 'Discovery' arrived off Cape Isabella on Sept. 9th, they discovered our cask of letters, and had the party who landed on that occasion examined the cairn also, they would then have found our record directing them to Littleton Island.

CHAPTER XI.

DRIVEN OUT OF SMITH SOUND.

I HAD not much time to decide what our next move should be, for the ice came driving round the cape as the wind increased from the southward, while to the south-east and east all was packed at a distance of a mile from us. To the northward we could do nothing, for a thick fog hung in that direction. I therefore bore away before the wind along the western shore towards Cape Sabine. In less than an hour we were again enveloped in a dense mist, through which we still groped our way, amongst loose floes and new ice, the land in the eastward as well as the land close on our port side being totally obscured.

By 11 A.M. we were again off Leconte Island, and the fog lifting, we could see from the crow's-nest that the pack extended in the south-west as far as visible and round into the land about Gale Point, and in one continuous body round by E.N.E., north and N.W., until it again closed in the land, and it appeared so close in the northward as completely to fill the straits, holding out not the slightest prospect of our proceeding in that direction. We were, in fact, in a pool of water formed by the late southerly storm, having eased the ice off the west land between Cape Isabella and Leconte Island, and upon which it was, now that the wind had subsided, again closing. To the eastward appeared a slack space apparently about the parallel in which we had passed through it on the previous night, although the weather was so thick at the time that it was impossible to say what our course had been. On watching this, however, it was evidently closing, but a lane farther

*

north seemed to offer a means of escape. If we had remained where we were, we should have been forced to the western shore or into Baird Inlet; to go north was impossible, and our only chance was to push back through the pack to the eastward, towards the water about Cape Alexander.

The fog soon shrouded the land again, and there was no time to be lost, so putting on full speed and setting all canvas we worked through the lead first north, then E.N.E. round to S.E. into a closer pack of drifting ice, and by 4 P.M. we got back again into the east water off M'Cormick Bight.

I consulted the officers as to our future movements, and called upon them to give me their opinions in writing as to our position. They hardly had a chance of deliberating, for we were forced to keep the ship moving to prevent our being hopelessly beset; and whilst they were writing their opinions the ship was being driven towards the only visible clear water in the eastward. With the natural sanguine feelings of youth, and with all the gallantry of naval officers, their opinions evidently were that we ought to endeavour to reach Cape Sabine at least, if that were possible; but that it would be madness to remain beset in this pack, or to attempt to push northward in it unless my intentions were to winter In all this I quite agreed, excepting that even if we could reach Cape Sabine it would be merely a proof of our having done our best, as no result could be expected beyond a day's later news of the outward voyage of the Polar ships. For if Captain Stephenson had sent a sledge party down in the spring with despatches, it would have had orders to proceed to Cape Isabella, and thence, if the straits were passable, to Littleton Island; and it was quite out of the question that they would have stopped short at Cape Sabine when their principal object in travelling at all would be to get those letters which they might hope to find deposited at Cape Isabella or Littleton Island.

I would, however, of course have gone to Cape Sabine if it had been possible, but in the meantime I had to act, and the only direction in which we could move was to the eastward. Had we hesitated we must either have been driven on the west shore, or allowed ourselves to be completely beset, and carried away with the main pack to the south-westward. Finding the ship once more under command, and again close into our harbour, I ran in, but on entering we found the inner harbour already full of loose ice, and were compelled to bring up in the bay outside, although the ground appeared hard and uneven, and the bay exposed to seaward.

We held on quietly enough all night, and on the 26th of August our sportsmen again went on shore and brought off about twenty hares. The birds had all departed save a solitary brood of ducks, which for some cause appeared to be very backward. They were guarded by two old birds, and I did not molest them, as they now appeared our only companions in these waters.

At 5 A.M. the wind again arose from the S.S.W., blowing in squalls, and by six the ice began to appear off the entrance, driving to the northward, and also closing on the land. I was preparing a depôt of provisions to place either here or at Littleton Island; but as soon as I could get every one on board I was obliged to steam out to prevent our being shut in altogether. Arriving outside we found a strong S.S.W. wind, and the S.W. pack coming in and already touching Sunrise Point and Littleton Island; so I got into the bight north of Cape Alexander, and dodged the ship all day and all night between the point of the cape and the glacier, in the water which still remained open. We might have got out close round the cape and to the southward along the land, but I did not wish to leave the straits so long as there remained the slightest chance of a change for the better, or of any boat party or the ships themselves arriving.

On the 27th of August it blew hard all night, with snow
squalls. I still hung on under Cape Alexander. The ice had
entered Foulke Fiord and Harbour, and jammed upon Littleton
and Sunrise Point. Two floes had already gone into
M'Cormick Bight and blocked the entrance, so that had we
remained there we could not have come out. The S.W. pack
was coming in apace, and in that direction round towards the
southern shore no water was visible where hitherto we had
always an open way ; but close in shore there still remained
a lead past Sutherland Island. The pack was now only three-
quarters of a mile from Cape Alexander, and we were forced
to make a move unless we wished to be jammed in Hartstene
Bay. The wind was increasing and another southerly storm
evidently at hand, so I forced the ship through the pack
to the southward as preferable to the shore lead ; and by
3 P.M. we got into a large space of water. We saw no more ;
the storm burst upon us with awful fury, and dense snow-
drifts. All that night we were going with the engines and
reefed fore-and-aft canvas, tacking incessantly as the pack
or bergs were reported on either hand ; a breaking sea
continually dashing over the ship, which proved that although
we had the ice to west and south-west, yet there was open
water in the south.

On the 28th the gale increased with such a blinding snowdrift that we could not see more than a few cables' length from
the ship. We continued with steam and the fore-and-aft
canvas, tacking about every quarter of an hour. The storm
lasted till one o'clock, when the sky suddenly cleared, the wind
moderated, and the sun burst out with great brilliancy, so
suddenly and unexpectedly as quite to cause a curious sensa-
tion in the change from darkness and gloom and snow to the
strong glare and warmth. Our decks were full of snow,
although we had been constantly clearing them. On going
aloft, we found that we were about ten miles south-west from

Cape Alexander. The ice extended in a pack from the cape round by north to south-west as far as visible, and we had been beating along its edge, and between it and a chain of icebergs to the eastward of us. In the southward, round to S.E. towards Murchison Sound, the sea was all clear, and along the eastern land there appeared to be a mass of bergs and grounded ice with loose floes. I could not see that the ice was actually touching Cape Alexander, but I could see no appearance of water off the cape, and I suspected that the S.W. pack had been driven into Hartstene Bay, and would not again move off until a strong north wind. We were, therefore, completely driven out of Smith Straits by the ice coming in, and in fact the whole of the ice from the southward appeared to have been driven north this year by the incessant southerly storms.

To return now was out of the question, unless to force the ship into Pandora Harbour and remain out for the winter; and I could not finally decide upon this point, until I had made arrangements, possibly at Upernivik, for communicating with the Admiralty. The Polar ships, if not under weigh, would not move until next season. It was far too late for any boat expedition to arrive southward.

Personally, I felt as if I had been overtaken by some sudden misfortune, for although I was aware of the fact that very soon we must leave the straits or be frozen in, yet the extreme anxiety and constant attention to the safety of the ship, and to our efforts to regain Cape Isabella, had so engrossed my mind that when the actual time arrived and we were outside the straits, with the ice already closed in behind us, and it was necessary to decide what we were to do, I could hardly realize the position.

CHAPTER XII.

VISIT TO THE ARCTIC HIGHLANDERS.

On the 28th of August, in the evening, we began to shape our course southwards. My poor crew, who had had such a buffeting, and were almost looking forward to going into snug winter quarters, soon began to speculate among themselves, and many were the inquiries of our civilian officers; but I must say that the men did not appear to brighten up at the idea of our return home which began to dawn upon them. They were as quiet and sober in their manner as they always had been, and were ready to carry out any orders they received.

All the night of the 28th, and the morning of the 29th, we slowly steamed southward in our iceless sea. The S.W. pack gradually receded as we drew towards Hakluyt Island, and on the morning of the 29th we had the most lovely weather, with a light S.E. wind, a brilliant sun, and a calm, smooth, and iceless sea. We were in another climate, which seemed almost tropical to us, and was in strange contrast to the appearance of the land, which was completely covered with snow by the late storm.

We had watched the tall spire on Hakluyt Island all night. Coming from the north, it looks like a gigantic cairn; but on a nearer approach it was seen to be a pinnacle of rock; probably gneiss, which ascends abruptly from the summit of the island. Passing close round the island, and also along the south shore of Northumberland Island, we stood towards Bardin Bay, as I wished to have an interview with the natives whom I expected to find there.

Standing towards the bay we soon observed a summer tent,

and, on a nearer approach, we could detect some people running backwards and forwards as if to attract our attention. We hauled into the bay, sounding carefully; but before we arrived off the encampment, which was on the east arm of the bay, the water shoaled to eleven, ten, seven, and then six fathoms, and at the same moment a reef just above the water was seen close ahead. Observing that the water was also breaking between us and the shore, we backed out and lay-to at the entrance of the bay. I immediately went away with the officers, and Anthone in his kayak, on a visit to the natives. They came down to meet us on the rocks, and I was surprised to notice how strong and well they all appeared. They showed no signs of fear, and were remarkably pleasing in their manner. We shook hands all round, and presented them with about 60 lb. of walrus meat. They consisted of one family apparently : a chief, who was not more than twenty-six, two young lads, an old woman, one young woman (the chief's wife), and a young girl, her sister, besides two children about ten years old. They invited us to their tents, which were made, as usual, of skins, with the poles of wood. Several bear-skins and reindeer skins were lying inside for their bedding. Many articles of wood and iron were inside, and lying about I noticed a ship's bucket, half of a mahogany table, with some brass studs, parts of an iron harpoon, pieces of a saw, and various other tools; also a Greenlander's kayak paddle much ice-worn, and a piece of a deal case marked " Limejuice, Leith." On questioning them, through Anthone, they said that all the wood in their possession was found at different times in the bay, where it had come in with the tide, and the iron had been amongst them a long time. They knew nothing of the 'Polaris' or of any white men, but said that some years ago a white man came with a dog sledge to Northumberland Island, to which they pointed. This, I think, must refer in some way to Dr. Hayes or Petersen. They also said that one of the

natives on Northumberland Island saw two ships go northward
last summer. I asked them if they wanted any food, as
I had about four tons of walrus meat in the 'Pandora,' but
they said that they had plenty, having had a good season with
white whales and seals in the bay. On my inquiring for some
narwhal horns, the chief at once sent off a boy to some huts
near the point, and he brought back four, which he said were
all they had, and gave them to me.

I presented them with six large knives, a large saw, some
packets of needles and thread, with all of which they seemed
delighted. The only thing they asked for was a gimlet and a
piece of wood like a boat's oar to make spears with; and on
the chief's going on board I gave him a fifteen-foot ash oar and
a plank. Combs, scissors, &c., were also sent to the ladies by
the officers, and they all seemed delighted. They offered everything we looked at, and would have readily given me everything
I asked for. I even asked if they would let me have some
of their fine dogs, and they immediately said " *Ap*," meaning
yes; so I took three away, and gave them five of ours in
exchange. I was anxious for these dogs, as they are trained to
hunt the bear, and are, I suppose, the finest sledge dogs in the
world. I also got a stone cooking pot, made of soapstone,
beautifully cut out, and a piece of their freestone, with which
they obtain a light by striking together over some burnt moss.
Only one of their winter storehouses was in use for habitation,
the others empty, and one used as a carpenter's shop, in which
they had been making some spears and hunting gear, and
draining off some oil from some fresh skins into well-made
buckets of walrus hide. They looked fat and happy, with
very good manners. I asked them if they would all come
with me to better climes farther south, but they declined, and
I could not induce one of the lads even to come, although they
showed no fear, and behaved just as if quite accustomed to
seeing *kablunas*, or white people.

NATIVES OF BARDIN BAY, WHALE SOUND.

CHAPTER XIII.

BACK AT UPERNIVIK.

WE passed close round Cape Parry during the night of August the 29th, with light easterly winds, and on the morning of the 20th were off Booth Bay. At noon we were off Saunders Island, and thence passing close to Wolstenholme Island we coasted down from Cape Athol to the Petowak Glacier. The sea was clear of ice to close into the shore. I intended to have stopped near the north end of the glacier and thence to have passed inside the Conical Rock to Cape Dudley Digges and Cape York; but a swell was setting in from the southward, and the threatening appearance of the weather denoted the approach of another southerly gale.

By 6 P.M. we were close off the Conical Rock, and the wind began to rise, until at midnight it blew a whole gale from the S.S.E.

All day and night of the 31st there was a continuous storm from the southward, with incessant heavy rain and thick weather. We could see but a little distance from the ship, and had constantly to avoid the icebergs. A heavy and breaking sea kept our decks continually afloat. Altogether it was miserable weather, and no progress.

During the 1st and 2nd of September[1] there were continued south winds, with thick weather and a nasty breaking sea. The ship was thoroughly damp and wet throughout. We were beating to windward, and saw nothing excepting icebergs since the evening of the 30th, when just off the Petowak Glacier and the Conical Rock. It, however, cleared a little at noon to-day,

---

[1] During the 1st and 2nd the 'Alert' and 'Discovery' were off Cape Hawke.

the 2nd, and we found by observation that we were in lat. 75° 37' N., and subsequent sights for time gave us our long. 68° 37' W. We had not seen a particle of floe-ice. On the 3rd of September there were still S. and S.W. winds. We kept under canvas, as it would have been a useless waste of coals to steam against this southerly sea.

On the 4th of September there were light airs and calms—altogether the finest day we had had since we had been in Baffin's Sea. We continued under canvas, and by noon were in lat. 74° 35' N., long. 64° 5' W., having made thirty-nine miles S. 87' E. since the day before. A great many icebergs were in sight all round; no floe-ice; sea smooth; occasional flights of ducks going due south; a few looms and rotches with the younger birds in the water, also mallemokes in company.

The 5th of September was a lovely day, calm and clear, with a bright warm sun and smooth sea. The icebergs which surrounded us appeared to have been tremendously washed and smashed up. We passed through the débris of one this morning, and took in about three tons of it for water. Lat. 74° 18', long. 63° 42'. As yet we had seen nothing of the middle ice, although a constant look-out was kept for it. It being quite calm in the afternoon we commenced steaming towards Upernivik.

On the 6th of September I was still steering to the S.E. towards Sanderson's Hope, as I intended to go to Upernivik; and if we were so fortunate as to find the Danish ship still there, I intended seriously to consider the project of sending home an officer and four or five men with news of our proceedings, and then to return northward with the 'Pandora' to have another look at the entrance to Smith Sound, or to push into harbour there and winter. The last Danish ship usually leaves Upernivik in the beginning or middle of September. I had hoped to have reached there in a few days, but we had now been nine days since we were driven out of Smith Sound on the 28th of August. There was, however, every probability of our reaching the port in two more days. Our latitude observed was 73° 19′ N., long. 61° 30′ W., so we had made only seventy-four miles S. 73′ E. since the day before.

Towards the afternoon we began to see indications of ice to the southward, and at 3 P.M., on passing some floe pieces, we observed a large bear seated on a small floe. I went away with Becker, and soon brought him to the ship, having shot him through the head with a single shot. He was a fine specimen, measuring nearly ten feet, with a good autumnal skin. We were not long in doubts about the ice, for by 4 P.M. we saw the main pack of the middle ice from south round to W.N.W. as far as visible. It appeared much broken at its outer edge, but beyond could be seen from the crow's-nest the same solid appearance, interspersed with icebergs, so well known to the navigators of those seas. At the time we had a light N.E. wind, with a clear sky, and were running under canvas. Had the weather been thick, with a gale blowing from the northward, we should in all probability have dashed right into the pack. Skirting along the edge of the ice to the S.E. we found that we were still in the east water, and were able to continue our course without interruption.

On the 6th of September we passed an immense number of icebergs of all sizes during the night, as we ran under reefed topsails, and by daylight of the 7th we could see Sanderson's Hope quite distinctly. By noon we came to the outermost of the Woman's Islands, threaded our way through between them and the reefs, and arrived off Upernivik at 5 P.M. Governor Thygesen came on board, and informed us that the last Danish ship had left for home on the 16th of August, and that there was now no chance of sending to England this year. I consequently went round into the harbour on the north side of the island, and moored there.

*

M

It was now necessary to decide upon my plans, and seeing no prospect of communicating with England I ordered the ship to be watered and refitted for sea.

During the three following days we remained in harbour refitting and resting the crew. I was still undecided what to do, as it was not yet too late to return northward if we could only get into our harbour in Smith Sound; but then it appeared to me that we could do no good, and might only embarrass the Admiralty by our absence, as I could not possibly communicate with them without going home. After well weighing the matter in my mind, I considered it best, from every point of view, that we should return to England, in order that the Admiralty might have the advantage of the knowledge we had acquired of the coast and harbour in Hartstene Bay, and the services of Arbuthnot and Pirie should they require them for the ship of next year. I had, moreover, no reason to suppose that Captain Nares had altered his programme in any way, or could in any way be dependent upon us. The main object appeared to be for the relief ship to arrive with certainty at her destination next season.

There was still a remote chance that Captain Nares, having finished his work, might yet come out with his ships, although we could not return into Smith Sound on the 28th of August. If he came out we should possibly hear of the ships at Disco, where I intended to touch to discharge our Eskimo, Anthone. For my part, I thought that Captain Nares had not attempted to come south; and the fact of our finding no news at either Cape Isabella or Littleton Island was a proof that they were all right, and had no cause to change the plans which he had so distinctly laid down in his communication with the Admiralty. It was, however, with anything but a cheerful feeling that I ordered the ship to be dismantled of her ice gear, boats, and crow's-nest, and the deck-load of provisions, always kept at hand in the ice, to be placed below. It was tantamount to saying that we were homeward bound, and the crew all felt it to be so, although I did not announce the fact to them. Indeed, I never felt more reluctance to return home than on this occasion.

We found the good people of Upernivik preparing for the long winter, and the hunters all hoping for the ice to arrive that the seals might come within their reach, for they were really destitute of all food, and the great junks of walrus meat and bear flesh which festooned our rigging, was a sight which gladdened their hearts. We gave away about three tons of it to the different heads of families, and, fortunately for us, they seemed to prefer it according to its degree of decomposition, thus enabling us to keep for ourselves and our dogs the best and freshest parts. We had the usual dancing in the evening, and smoking and drinking of coffee in the daytime, whenever we went near the settlement; but all our attempts at finding out if there was any chance of getting up a hunting excursion failed completely. We got no encouragement from anyone. The seals had not yet arrived, the deer were too far away inland, and, in fact, when a ship is in port, it seems impossible for anyone to suggest anything beyond the usual smoking, drinking coffee, and making presents to the inhabitants.

I was much interested by the Governor telling me that a reindeer had been shot quite lately, having a brand mark T on the forehead. He had sent the skin to Copenhagen, and I have no doubt some light will be thrown upon the extraordinary wanderings of these animals. Can it have come from Spitzbergen? The natives say that it is the first time that such a mark has ever been found on a deer.

The summer at Upernivik had been very stormy, with constant southerly gales, and very much as we experienced the weather farther north. They considered it a very bad season for ice navigation, and that the pack ice was very near the coast; and indeed we had seen it only about fifty miles to the north-west the day before we arrived. There was also a rumour that a steamship had been seen passing southward, off Proven, on August 18, from which they thought that some of the whale ships might have failed in crossing Melville Bay. This, however, I did not believe to be the case, or we should assuredly have seen something of them when beset in the bay.

CHAPTER XIV.

MEETING WITH THE POLAR SHIPS.

WE left Upernivik at 6.30 in the evening of the 11th of September[1] with fine clear weather, and steamed clear of all the islands, and then put the ship under canvas for the night, as it was so dark that we could not expect to make much progress through the icebergs until daylight.

On the 13th of September the wind increased to a fresh gale from the northward towards noon, when we were in lat. 70° 51′ N., long. 56° 32′ W., and in the afternoon the weather was very thick. We stood on to the southward until dark, when we hove-to under fore-and-aft canvas.

On the 14th there was thick fog and mist, and it was blowing a gale from the N.N.W. Dodging under low sail, and sometimes running off to the southward, but not being able to see any distance, and wishing to stop at Godhavn, I could not run for the land. We passed many icebergs and wash pieces. Our latitude by reckoning 69° 56′, long. 57° 20′. There was a high breaking sea all the afternoon, and we ran for four hoûrs to E.S.E. until dark, when a dense snow storm arose and continued through the night. The ship was hove-to, with the head to westward, under low canvas.

On the 15th of September the weather cleared at 8 A.M., and the wind and snow having abated, we got up steam and proceeded towards Godhavn, passing Disco Fiord and Laxe Bay in the evening, and arriving off the harbour about 10 P.M.

[1] The Arctic ships passed Cape Sabine on the 9th of September, and Captain Markham landed at Cape Isabella on the same day. He found the letters and papers left by me on the 6th of August. On the 11th they were off the entrance of Whale Sound.

It was intensely dark, and we could not even see the rocks under the high land, so, having fired a gun and rocket, and it being answered from the shore, I hove-to until daylight.

We entered and anchored off the settlement on the 16th. I was glad to find here Mr. Krarup Smith, the Inspector of North Greenland, who was very kind in offering his services in any way. He informed me that the last ship had not yet left Egedesminde, but that he was just sending off his letters for her, and she would sail on the following morning. Had I known this on my arrival at Upernivik, I would have sent Arbuthnot here in a boat for a passage home, with despatches, and then had another look northward. It was now too late, and I feared that there was nothing left but to prepare for our homeward voyage. I determined to remain at Godhavn a few days, upon the remote chance of the Polar ships yet arriving.

I left Godhavn on the 21st,[1] with a light N.E. wind, the weather being very fine and the sea calm, with many icebergs in sight.

On the 22nd there was a light northerly wind. On the 23rd and 24th there was beautiful weather, calm and light airs and nice smooth sea. The ship was under canvas, but making little way. We tried the fishing lines for halibut, but caught nothing, though we shot 100 kittiwakes. They are quite equal to the Bordeaux pigeon if carefully skinned and stewed. The Greenland coast was in sight all the time. It was so clear, and calm, and bright, that we could fancy we were in a tropical sea instead of within the Arctic Circle and the Equinox passed since the 22nd. The nights were, however, intensely dark, or appeared so, after our late experience in the far north.

During the following days we had nothing but light baffling air, and the weather, which had been lately so fine and clear, now became thick and overcast with a constant fog.

---

[1] The 'Alert and Discovery arrived at Godhavn on the 25th.

We made but little progress, and I would have steamed part of the time, only that we had pumped the water out of the boilers, and they, with the engines and bunkers, were having a regular clean up and refit after seventy-seven days that our fires were alight, with steam always at hand.

At noon on the 1st of October, we suddenly met the Spitzbergen ice in large streams. It was very heavy with a tremendous surf breaking amongst it. I then close-reefed and ran out to the westward, following its edge; but by dark we could see no end to it, and a gale coming in from the southward with rain and sleet, I put the ship under very low canvas and lay-to with head to the E.N.E.

I had been much surprised the last few days at the amazing number of bergs and wash pieces that we had passed, and I had also been forewarned by the lowness of the temperature and the freezing of our sails and ropes. The last few days also the sea surface-water stood at 33° to 34°; but I certainly did not expect to find the ice here and in such quantities. It is generally thought that it never extends beyond Godthaab to the northward; but I suppose the extraordinary prevalence of south winds this season must have driven it up and out to the N.W. It is most alarming to meet with, especially with a gale approaching, as it is too close to enter and too open for protection from the heavy sea, and is of that heavy oceanic character which renders it most dangerous to strike.

On the 2nd it was blowing a gale from the S.E. We had a dreadful night of wind and sleet and fog, and a very high breaking sea. We lay-to all night, and occasionally fell in with heavy floe pieces and bergs, but luckily escaped them all. Our position was 65° N., long. by D. R. 54° 30' W. We were all day standing to S.S.W. under storm sails, and occasionally using steam to clear the ice.

In the night it fell calm, and a thick fog came on. All

night and all the morning of the 3rd we could hear the roaring of the sea and surf as it broke upon the ice, but we could see nothing—it was dark and thick, the principal sound being in the S.E. We lay still, using steam only now and then to clear the ice. In the forenoon at eight o'clock a light wind sprung up from the northward, and we proceeded under all canvas, steering S.S.W., and passing much ice; but as the sea was fast subsiding and the weather promising to be fine I felt no more anxiety, and we ran all day, and by 6 P.M. we began to lose sight of all floe-ice, but met occasional bergs. Our screw was hoisted, and we continued on S. by W.

On the 15th of October we were in lat. 55° 20' N., long. 46° 31' W. Ever since the 4th we had experienced the most awful weather. It rained in torrents with a high confused sea. On the 8th, 9th, and 10th, we had a heavy gale, and the barometer on the morning of the 12th, in lat. 57° 47' N., long. 51° W., went down to 28·66, when we had another easterly gale, which lasted with several slight intervals until the 15th, when the mercury rose to 29·40, the air cleared, and we had a strong N.W. wind. Certainly this is a stormy sea, and it seemed that if the wind once set in from the S.E. and E. in the neighbourhood of Cape Farewell, and between the lands of Greenland and Labrador, the weather might be expected to be very unsettled for many days, accompanied with constant heavy squalls and rain, and a high irregular pyramidal sea.

In consequence of the weather we were so much delayed in getting out of Davis Straits, that although we sailed two days earlier this year than last from Disco, yet we were already eleven days behind; and in last year's passage home we were at this date running up the English Channel, from which we are now distant 1497 miles. We had much, however, to be thankful for, as we were all well, and had carried nothing away or done the least damage to the ship, and we were now looking forward to a favourable run home.

Our standard mercurial barometer fell gradually from the 9th until the 12th, when it stood at 28·66, the lowest reading I ever saw excepting in a tropical cyclone. The mercury remained at this depression with but slight variation until the 15th, when it gradually rose after the previous noon and until the previous midnight, when it rose quickly, and by 8 A.M. we had a hard, clear N.W. wind. The sea ran principally from the E.N.E. whichever way the wind blew, and caused the sea to pitch and tumble in a most alarming manner.

The 16th of October was an eventful day. This morning at daylight two ships were reported astern, steering the same course as ourselves, and from their appearance, though hull down, I took them to be the Hudson Bay Company's vessels, as they were evidently not whalers by the course they were steering. Later we could see the boats' davits and boats; but the wind was tantalizingly calm; and it was not until they both gave a sheer and thus a side view, that we saw by the position of their funnels, &c., that they were the 'Alert' and 'Discovery.'

We were about seven miles from them in the forenoon, and a breeze springing up from the southward we steered close to them, when the 'Alert' made signals that an impenetrable Polar sea had been reached, and that the sledges had attained the highest northern latitude. I replied with congratulations on the success of the expedition.

Our place of this strange and happy meeting was in lat. 54° 38′ N., long. 44° 30′ W.

During the night of the 16th, it blew hard from the S.E. with heavy rain. We carried on with single reefs in topsails and fore-and-aft sails, and by daylight the Polar ships were hull down on our lee quarter.

On the 17th we ran down and exchanged a series of signals with the 'Alert.' On the 18th there was a strong S.S.W. wind, with squalls. We were still in company with the Polar ships, but they were rather outsailing us. Towards evening the wind suddenly freshened to a hard gale, with torrents of rain, and at eight it was blowing so heavy that we furled all square canvas.

On the 19th the weather was still threatening with an irregular sea. At daylight we saw the 'Discovery,' but could see nothing of the 'Alert.' Lat. 55° 39' N., long. 35° 48' W. In the afternoon the 'Discovery' was showing signals, but too distant to distinguish, perhaps to us or to her consort.

The night set in with torrents of rain; wind from N. to N.N.E., sea heaving in high pyramidal waves, sky fiery red in the westward at sunset, and every indication of an approaching storm.

CHAPTER XV.

HOMEWARD BOUND.

ON the 20th of October it rained in a perfect sheet all night, the wind flying about, and the ship very uneasy until 8 A.M., when I observed a small bright opening in the south-west. The barometer, which had been rapidly falling during the night, stood at 28·36, and I was prepared for a storm. I now took in all canvas, excepting the two topsails which were storm-reefed, and the inner jib, and had everything secured, and yards braced round for a S.W. wind. At 8.15 the storm burst suddenly upon us, and increased, so rapidly that we had only just time to roll up our topsails and get the jib down, and scud under bare poles until we could set a close-reefed fore staysail. As the wind increased, so the barometer began to rise rapidly, and by nine o'clock we had a complete hurricane. I kept the ship dead before the wind, expecting every minute that our staysail would burst; but we held on, and we were fortunately, by good steering, able to continue to run. At ten we were pooped, but not very badly, the sea, however, smashed in our port round-house and knocked our gunner (Mitchell) down; but he escaped with a severe contusion on one of his legs. The wind now blew in such gusts as to shake the masts in an extra-ordinary manner, although no canvas was set on them, and the sea was one mass of foam and spray, and curled up in steep walls.

By eleven the sea had got more foot, or base, and ran higher, so that it was not nearly so dangerous, and the weight of the gale had arrived. We then set about three feet of the fore topsail and scudded more easily. At noon we were in lat. 55° 19′, long. 33° 49′, so that the hurricane occurred in about lat. 55° N., long. 34° 10′ W. After noon the violence of the storm began to decrease, and we were able to set the main topsail close-reefed; and by evening it had settled down to a hard gale from the S.W., on which we made snug sail for the night and hauled the ship more to the eastward. The barometer had also risen so much that all anxiety was over.

At the commencement of the storm the force of the wind was so great that it was difficult to get along the deck, and the rain and spray so enveloped the ship that it was impossible to distinguish between the two; but at 9.30 A.M. the sun appeared, and the dense clouds began to open, and I think that about that hour the continuous rain ceased, although we had incessant squalls accompanied with hail.

Altogether this was a most remarkable storm, and I felt much interested in comparing notes with the Polar ships on arriving in England. They could not have been far distant, although we saw nothing of them, nor did we see them again. I cannot allow this opportunity to pass without expressing my opinion of the value of the patent reefing gear—Colling's and Pinkney's—with which our topsails were fitted. It is the most beautiful invention I know at sea, and enables the sail to be furled at a minute's notice, or to be enlarged or reduced immediately from the deck without the necessity of sending a single man aloft.

On the 21st of October the wind veered more westerly, enabling us to lay our course under close-reefed sails. The weather was altogether finer this morning, and we gradually made all sail. Latitude observed 55° 26′ N., long. 30° 16′ W. In the afternoon the wind hauled to the southward with squalls of rain. On the 22nd there was a strong S.S.E. wind lasting throughout the night, with lightning. The ship was standing to the eastward all day under snug sail, but as much as we could safely carry.

The 28th of October was a lovely day, the sea smooth and a brilliant sun; temperature in the shade 57°, and we felt as if we were in the middle of summer. We took advantage of this beautiful weather to dry all our clothing and bedding, which had become saturated with damp; and the 'Pandora' looked like a scene in Rag Fair. The comfort of having once more a dry deck, and of being able to open all windows and hatchways, was incalculable. We were, however, becalmed; and unable to bear the suspense any longer, we lowered our propeller at 9 A.M., and steamed all day.

At 3 P.M. of the 29th we made land northward of Dingle Bay, and soon saw the Skelligs. On the 30th we steamed slowly towards the Mizen Head, passing it at half a mile, and rounded-to off Crookhaven, where we signalled a boat, and I telegraphed to the Admiralty. We received but little news from the simple fishermen; but they informed us that the 'Alert' had touched on the 27th at Valentia, and that Captain Nares had landed, and also that a ship answering the description of the 'Discovery' had been cruising the previous day off the Fastnet. We bore away at noon under steam and fore-and-aft canvas; wind light from E.N.E., and being able to steam only about three knots. We were having quite summer weather, and the sea was smooth; and as we passed out between Cape Clear and the Fastnet we had a splendid view of this romantic coast, and saw a fleet of boats fishing around the Fastnet Rock.

We crossed to Scilly on the 31st with a fine fresh N.N.E. wind, passing many outward-bound ships, and by 6 P.M. we had passed north of Scilly and the Seven Stones. Steering then between the Wolf and the Longship, we were off the Lizard at 1 A.M. on November 1st, and finding that the wind was coming down fresh from the eastward, I went into Falmouth at 8 A.M., and there took in twenty tons of coal, as we could not get at our own on board without removing a great many stores off the lower deck.

At Falmouth we got the newspapers, giving us further information of the proceedings of the Polar ships. We passed Portland at 1 P.M., the Needles at eight, arriving at Cowes at 10 P.M., and entered Portsmouth harbour on the 3rd of November, 1876.

APPENDIX.

CONTENTS OF THE APPENDIX.

———◦◦———

I.

Papers relating to the First Voyage of the 'Pandora.'

1875.

II.

Papers relating to the Second Voyage of the 'Pandora.'

1876.

*

APPENDIX.

I.

PAPERS RELATING TO THE FIRST VOYAGE OF THE
'PANDORA.'

1875.

A.

LETTERS to the 'TIMES' from the REV. S. HAUGHTON and CAPTAIN ALLEN YOUNG, on the TIDAL BARRIER.

To the Editor of the 'Times.'

"SIR,—In the year 1857, when M'Clintock was about to set out on his search for Franklin in the 'Fox,' I called his attention to the probability that there is a permanent tidal ice-barrier all through the Arctic Archipelago, caused by the still water occasioned by the meeting of the Davis's Strait and Behring's Strait tides from the Atlantic and Pacific Oceans; and I ventured at that time to draw on the chart the most probable line of junction of the Atlantic and Pacific tides, in the portion of the Archipelago which he was about to search. The 'Erebus' and 'Terror' were beset and perished within a very short distance of the tidal barrier line so drawn.

"It is well known from the experience of Collinson and M'Clure that vessels can enter the Arctic Archipelago through Behring's Strait and sail to the eastward and north-eastward, to within some fifty or sixty miles of places which can be easily reached from the Atlantic side through Lancaster Sound.

"The ships from Behring's Strait always find themselves in the Pacific tide, and the ships from Lancaster Sound always find themselves in the Atlantic tide, but no ship has yet crossed the tidal ice-barrier, and passed into the open water of the other ocean, and I believe no ship ever will do so.

"The recent voyage of the 'Pandora' is simply a repetition of the experiment so often made unsuccessfully to cross this barrier. The 'Pandora' found no difficulty, having reached Lancaster Sound, in pushing on to Beechey Island, and afterwards in making her way down Peel Sound (Franklin Channel), along the very route traversed by the unfortunate 'Erebus' and 'Terror,' but as soon as she had reached La

Roquette Island, at the western entrance of Bellot Strait, she met the ice-barrier twenty-five feet thick and fifty miles wide. If the 'Pandora' had ventured into this barrier, she would have shared the fate of the 'Erebus' and 'Terror,' but she would not have made the North-West Passage.

" Before the 'Alert' and 'Discovery' sailed in this year, I wrote to Captain Nares, giving him my reasons for thinking that he would find the tidal ice-barrier after passing through Smith Sound at this side of the North Pole, and I instructed several officers of the expedition in a method of telling quickly whether the ships are in the Atlantic tide or in the Pacific tide.

" If my opinion should turn out to be correct, the wisest course the ships could adopt after meeting the tidal ice-barrier would be to keep well to the southward of it, and trust the entire chances of the expedition to sledge travelling, by means of which it would be probably an easy matter to reach the North Pole.

" I am, Sir, yours faithfully,
" SAMUEL HAUGHTON.

" TRINITY COLLEGE, DUBLIN, *Nov.* 1."

To the Editor of the 'Times.'

" SIR,—Will you allow me to make the following remarks upon Professor Haughton's letter in the 'Times' of to-day?

" It is well known that the learned Professor has given great attention to the universal tidal action, and especially to the tidal wave in the Arctic Seas, and there is no one living whose opinions are more valued. I do not think, however, that it was a tidal barrier which arrested the 'Pandora' on her late voyage, but an accumulation of ice, the result of an exceptional season, and the extraordinary prevalence of strong N.W. winds, which drove the Polar pack through M'Clintock Channel, impinging it on the Boothian coast, and blocking the southern part of Franklin Channel, and thus prevented the last winter's ice in those straits from breaking up. The N.W. winds would be as much in favour of clearing the way of the Government expedition going north from Baffin's Sea as they were against my prospect of proceeding south from Barrow Strait, and I trust that Captain Nares has this season reached a very high latitude without meeting any tidal ice-barrier in that direction.

" There is no evidence to prove by which route the 'Erebus' and 'Terror' reached the point at which they were finally beset, and in the absence of such proof I consider that, without detracting from the discoveries of that great navigator, Sir John Franklin, the 'Pandora' may fairly claim to be the first ship ever known to have navigated through Peel's Strait to lat. 72° 8′, at the entrance to Franklin Channel, and thus to have added one more step in the right direction. I yet hope to make another attempt; and even again failing, I shall still hope on that some future navigator more fortunate than myself may prove the North-West Passage to be open for at least a short season in most years.

"I was on my late voyage fully alive to the great risk to which Professor Haughton alludes of entering the pack which we met. But we found it quite impossible to do so, and wherever we attempted it an impenetrable line of ice, without the slightest lane of water, presented itself to our view. And I quite agree with him that it would have been a very false manœuvre to have allowed our ship to be beset in such a position, and thus to have probably ended our voyage in a disaster.

"I am, Sir,
"Your very obedient servant,
"ALLEN YOUNG,
"Commander Arctic ship 'Pandora.'
"1, ST. JAMES'S STREET, S.W., Nov. 4."

B.

LETTER from ADMIRAL SIR RICHARD COLLINSON, K.C.B., to MISS CRACROFT.

"October 12th, 1875.

"MY DEAR MISS CRACROFT,—I enclose Young's letters to M'Clintock, which I received this morning. He would like to have them back when you have done with them.

"The outward passage has been so long that I have no doubt the loss of daylight will prevent them attempting Peel Sound this season. It would be madness to winter anywhere in the neighbourhood of Bellot Strait on that side. I do not believe there is an indentation either on North Somerset—W. side—or the Prince of Wales' Island, that the ice does not move in the winter, and it will not do to expose the 'Pandora' to a second edition of what the 'Terror' underwent in Hudson's Bay. The tide will be the means by which the passage will be made; but the tide must be encountered with the advantage of daylight and a higher temperature.

"I shall not be surprised to see them in England before the end of the month.

"Yours very sincerely,
"R. COLLINSON."

II.

PAPERS RELATING TO THE SECOND VOYAGE OF THE 'PANDORA.'

1876.

C.

Mr. Allen Young to the Secretary of the Admiralty.

"Arctic Yacht 'Pandora,' R.Y.S.
"Cowes, *May* 29*th*, 1876.

" Sir,—I have the honour to acknowledge the receipt of their Lordships' Memorandum of the 16th instant, together with copies of the instrucions furnished to Captain Nares and other documents bearing on the subject of communication with the depôts of the Arctic Expedition, at the entrance of Smith Sound during this summer, a service which I have had the honour to accept at their Lordships' invitation.

" I have read and given my careful consideration to all these documents, and as their Lordships have not laid down the decided line of action they desire me to follow, I conclude that they leave it to my own judgment to carry out, so far as circumstances will admit, their general views consequent on Captain Nares' communications.

" I beg you will acquaint their Lordships, that while I gratefully accept and appreciate this mark of their confidence, I feel that it is proper, and that they will expect, that I should lay before them a statement of my own views on the service I am about to undertake, and of the course I propose to follow.

" Captain Nares states in his communication from Disco that his second in command, Captain Stephenson, will be directed to communicate in the spring of this year with a depôt at or near the entrance to Smith Sound, and perhaps again in the autumn.

" My duty then will be to land despatches and letters at this depôt, and to bring away any that I may find deposited there.

" My opinion is that if the Expedition reached any very considerable distance north in the summer of 1875, say as far as Hall's wintering place, then no attempt would be made to communicate with the depôt at the entrance of Smith Sound during the spring of this year, and in that event I should find no later letters than those which were probably deposited in August, 1875, on the way north, and only a few days' later intelligence than that which I brought to England from the Cary Islands on my return in October last year.

" Such a result as this, although it is quite possible to be all that I might be able to accomplish, would convey but little additional information to their Lordships and would probably not be very satisfactory to the public.

"As regards the possible communications from the Expedition in the autumn, their Lordships are aware that autumn travelling can only be undertaken after the summer navigation has closed and the sea is again frozen over, and then only to a limited extent.

" To receive such a communication, I should have to go into winter quarters at the end of this summer, and I should then be in no better position as regards bringing despatches to England than the Government ship which it is intended to despatch in 1877 (should the Expedition not return in the summer of this year).

" It is possible, however, that Captain Nares or Captain Stephenson may despatch a boat expedition to the depôt in the month of July this year, and, if so, it is of course possible that I may communicate with it. With this view I shall feel it incumbent on me to remain at the entrance of Smith Sound until the navigable season is well advanced, and I should hope during this detention to gain such information in regard to wintering places on either side, as would be useful to the ships to be despatched in the summer of 1877.

" Failing any communication with the Expedition up to that time, and if then too late to prosecute the objects of my own intended voyage to the west, I should return to England.

" The preceding observations are based upon the supposition that Captain Nares reached the position which it was contemplated by the Arctic Committee that the ships might arrive at under favourable circumstances, and which there is good reason to believe they may have reached.

" If, on the other hand, they have been unable to penetrate further than from sixty to eighty miles within the entrance of the Sound, their communication with their depôt will be much more certain, and my chance of bringing information from them proportionately so. I earnestly trust, however, that this will not have been the case.

" Under any circumstances their Lordships may rely that no pains will be spared on my part to carry out their wishes, to which I shall consider all other things secondary.

"I shall observe the usual custom of communicating with their Lordships by all opportunities and of leaving records of my proceedings wherever I may be able to do so, after leaving the Danish settlements of Greenland. And in the event of my obtaining despatches from Captain Nares, or Captain Stephenson, I will take such means as will be best to ensure their arrival in England as speedily as possible.

"I have, &c.,

"ALLEN YOUNG, Lieut. R.N.R.,

" *Commander Arctic yacht ' Pandora.' "*

D.

The SECRETARY of the ADMIRALTY to MR. ALLEN YOUNG.

"ADMIRALTY, 31*st May*, 1876.

"SIR,—With reference to your letter of 29th instant and your telegram of this day, I am commanded by my Lords Commissioners of the Admiralty to inform you that they entirely concur in the views expressed in your letter, and their Lordships desire to leave it to your own judgment to determine the steps that will be most advisable for carrying out their general views consequent on the communications received from Captain Nares, of which copies were forwarded to you on the 16th instant.

"I am, &c.,

(Signed)　　　"ROBERT HALL."

E.

OFFICIAL REPORT made to the SECRETARY of the ADMIRALTY by CAPTAIN ALLEN YOUNG.

" *November*, 1876.

"I have the honour to forward you, for the information of the Lords Commissioners of the Admiralty, the following Report of my proceedings in the 'Pandora' subsequent to the 19th of July, the date of my last communication :—

"We left Upernivik the same evening, and passed the Duck Islands on the 21st, having been much embarrassed between the reefs and islands by a thick fog. We here met streams of ice, and the fog continuing, with a strong north-west wind, I made fast to a large floe, but the ship breaking adrift in the night, we stood to the north-east under low canvas, passing much ice and innumerable bergs.

" On the 22nd the wind changed to the southward, and the sky partially cleared. Wilcox Head bore east fifteen miles, and we commenced threading our way to the west-north-west.

" During that afternoon and night we had a fresh gale from southeast, with thick weather, and the barometer having fallen to 28·90, warned us of an approaching storm. We continued running under reefed sails through vast fields of ice, having frequently to alter our course, or bring the ship to the wind to clear the floes and bergs.

" On the following morning (the 23rd), finding that we were apparently entering the main pack, I came out again fifteen miles S.S.E. under steam, and, as the thick snow prevented our seeing any distance, I there made fast to a floe in what appeared to be a large space of water.

" We saw nothing more until the morning of the 24th, when I found that we were quite surrounded, but with much water in the southward, from which we were shut off by a barrier of about two miles in width. This was in latitude, by account, 75° 10′ N., longitude, by account, 62° 7′ W.

" No time was lost in endeavouring to effect our escape by forcing this block with all the steam we could command, and we were making gradual progress when the whole body of ice in which we were beset, drifting before the gale, came in contact with a group of grounded bergs, and caused the ship to be so severely nipped, that at 3 P.M. I ordered every preparation to be made in the event of our having to abandon her. Provisions, ammunition, camping and travelling gear, &c., were all made ready, the boats were loaded as far as possible at the davits, ready to be lowered at a moment's notice; the violence of the weather, and of the commotion in the ice, rendering it imprudent to put anything upon the floe until the worst should arrive.

" During all this time we continued blasting the ice around the ship with heavy charges, and thereby relieved her considerably at the points where she was most severely pressed. We were thus held in suspense until 8 P.M., when the bearings of the icebergs having altered, and the extreme pressure easing off, the ship came almost upright, and began to settle down to the proper level of flotation.

" In the meantime the ice had accumulated, and the storm continuing, we were drifted helplessly with the pack; and, owing to the constant snow and sleet, we saw but little more until the 27th, when the weather cleared, and we obtained observations for the first time since the 20th, placing us in lat. 75° 44′ N., long. 62° 20′ W. We had thus driven up into the heart of Melville Bay, and could see no water from the crow's-nest. The ice was closed tight up in every direction, and presented all the appearance of a winter's pack. It was a beautifully clear afternoon, and we had Capes Walker, Melville, the Peaked Hill, and the intervening glaciers all distinctly in view.

"On the 28th, the whole pack driving westward, and through some more grounded icebergs, a narrow lane of water formed in their wake, into which we managed to force the ship, and succeeded in making about five miles to the S.S.W., the continuous flights of the little auk passing and repassing having convinced me that the nearest open water lay in that direction. We were, however, unable to move the ship except in her dock to relieve her of projecting points, and the same night another storm commenced to blow furiously from the E.S.E., and the whole pack drove rapidly to the westward, carrying us through a line of bergs, nearly in collision with one of enormous size, which we had seen in the morning twelve miles to the westward of our position.

"On the 29th, the wind S.S.E., blowing a gale with snow, the pack was still driving to the westward. By the afternoon we could see from aloft some water in the S.W., but, although we made every effort, we were unable to move the ship until 7 P.M., when the wind changed to S.W. The ice began to slacken, and by putting on all steam we forced the ship into the water, and effected our escape by 9 P.M., in lat. 75° 50′ N., long. 64° 55′ W. Thence we stood away to the westward in a clear sea.

"During this detention we killed only one Polar bear, four seals, and some little auks.

"We passed Capes Dudley Digges and Athol as near as the off-lying ice would admit on the morning of the 31st, having been again hampered by thick weather, and by noon we were off Wolstenholme Island, when another gale commenced from the southward, and increased rapidly to almost hurricane force. Unable to obtain shelter on the coast from the number of bergs and wash pieces, we lay-to under storm canvas all night, unable to see any distance on account of the spray and snowdrift, and in order to avoid collision with the icebergs the ship had to be frequently kept away, and we were boarded by several heavy beam seas, which smashed our first whale-boat, filled the decks, and washed all our deck load adrift.

"On August 1 the gale moderated, and I steered for the S.E. Cary Island, as I was desirous of examining Captain Nares' depôt of provisions to enable me to report upon its condition. We arrived at the island at noon, and at 4 P.M., the sea having subsided sufficiently, Lieutenant Arbuthnot landed, and reported on his return at 7 P.M. that the depôt was found in good order and the cairn unvisited since I was there on the 10th of September last year.

" We now bore away to the northward, and with a fine clear night passed Hakluyt Island. The following forenoon, when in lat. 77° 46′ N., we made the pack on our port hand trending from south-west to north-east as far as visible in the direction of Cape Alexander. I had expected from the prevalence of southerly gales to find that much ice had been driven north this season, but I was not prepared to meet this great pack so soon or extending so far out from the west land in this position.

" We stood direct for Sutherland Island, and a party left the ship on our arrival, and returned at 11 P.M., having found a record of Captain Hartstene's, U.S. Navy, dated August 16, 1855, but no signs of the island having been subsequently visited.

" Passing Cape Alexander at midnight, the pack was lying two miles off with navigable water in Hartstene Bay, but the straits all full of heavy ice in the west and north.

" August 3.—As we approached Littleton Island we saw two cairns. The ice lay close on the south-western point, but apparently slack on the mainland, and in the narrow passage between the main and the island. I therefore steamed through the channel and anchored in a small opening between Littleton and M'Gary Islands.

" Having moored with warps to the ice-foot still attached to the rocks, Lieutenants Arbuthnot and Becker hurried on shore to search the cairns, and shortly after their departure the ice began driving from the westward through our anchorage, and so continually fouled our warps, although they were taken to the mastheads to clear it, that by 7 A.M. we were fairly driven out stern foremost, not having room to turn the ship round. I had in the meantime landed a boat and camping gear for our absentees, in the event of our being driven away from the island ; but having succeeded in lying close under the north-east point we had the satisfaction of seeing them crossing the hill, and shortly afterwards of receiving them on board. They brought a record, dated the 28th of July, 1875, from Captain Nares' cairn, and a closed letter addressed to C. Markham, Esq.

" It was evident from Captain Nares' record that we must next attempt to reach Cape Isabella, which, however, in the present condition of the ice—the straits being packed full in every direction—was quite impossible to do. I therefore decided to take advantage of the delay by examining the coast in Hartstene Bay, in accordance with their Lordships' desire that I should seek a harbour for the relief ship to be sent out in 1877, if the Polar Expedition did not return earlier.

" We first examined Julia's Glen, and thence sounded on to Port Foulke, but found deep water close up to the head. It is a mere indentation in the land, partially sheltered by three small islands, but exposed to the west and south-west. I cannot recommend it, unless at the close of the navigable season, for a very small ship, intending to winter, to run into the young ice and be frozen in immediately.

" Entering Foulke Fiord we got soundings from seventeen to seven fathoms, but with an irregular and rocky bottom, and thence deep water up to the small island, where the fast ice still remained across the fiord, to the Eskimo huts of Etah. This fast ice was too decayed to moor to, and the pack threatening to come in, we proceeded out of the fiord, and lay-to for the night in Julia's Glen.

" This fiord is also exposed to the westward, and were a ship to find an anchorage in the upper part and winter there, I think it might be late in the summer before the fast ice would break away and set her free.

" On August 4, blowing hard from the south-westward, pack closing the land, and already filling Port Foulke and Fiord, we stood round into M'Cormick Bight, and found regular soundings from fifteen to ten fathoms, and on passing the inner point we anchored in an excellent harbour, with seven fathoms water, and a good stiff mud bottom.

" I can strongly recommend this harbour, to which I gave the name of our ship, the 'Pandora,' being the first to visit it.

" It has every advantage, easy to enter, good holding ground, and sheltered from all points. A reef from Cape Kenrick, upon which the heavy ice grounds, gives protection from the westward. The only necessary precaution, if not intending to winter, would be to avoid being shut in late in the season, when young ice is forming, by the drift ice from outside.

" Here will be found game in abundance at this season; the surrounding hills are dotted with Arctic hares, appearing like snowballs on the luxuriant vegetation. On the northern cliff, immediately over the anchorage, there is a breeding-place of the little auk, which assemble there in thousands. Reindeer are in the neighbourhood, and eider fowl and black guillimots are numerous upon the water. I am confident that a ship arriving here early in August might, with organized hunting parties, obtain an ample supply of fresh food for the following winter.

" It blew a heavy gale all night of the 4th, with violent snow squalls over the high land, but we rode in perfect safety and comfort.

" On the 5th of August the weather moderated. Lieutenants Pirie,

Becker, and Beynen commenced a survey of the harbour, and I went upon the high land to view the straits. Some guns also went out to procure game.

" The prospect from Cape Kenrick was not very clear or encouraging ; the straits in the north-west and north round to Sunrise Point were full of heavy floes. A mist hung over the ice in the west, but I saw that the pack was loosened in the direction of Cape Isabella, so, hastily returning on board, we weighed anchor at 4 P.M. Our sportsmen, who hurried back on the recall being made, brought a quantity of hares and other game.

" We steered across the straits with a fresh north wind, passing through the pack, and with some difficulty keeping the direction, owing to the necessary deviations of our course and the weak horizontal force of our compasses ; but as we drew over on the west side the weather cleared, and having set our close-reefed topsails, we reached Cape Isabella at 3 A.M. on Sunday, August 6.

" We soon observed a large cairn on the summit, but as we had now a gale from the north, with the tide, or current, running four knots to the southward, and carrying blocks of ice past the rocks, it was six o'clock before we could place the ship in such a position as to enable the boat to land. Lieutenants Arbuthnot and Becker immediately left with their crew, fully provided with all necessary camping gear in case of need.

" I was somewhat puzzled how to act for the best with regard to our despatches and letters, Captain Nares having requested, at Littleton Island, that they might be landed at Cape Isabella, or carried as far north as a ship intended to go ; but as in the present condition of the straits, and at this early season, it was impossible to know what our future proceedings would be, or even if we could again visit the cape, and, moreover, the despatches not being in duplicate, I considered it for the best to land now the loose letters, which seemed to comprise some for nearly every member of the Expedition, and to reserve the sealed bags until the landing party returned with further information. These letters, therefore, were packed in a cask and sent in the boat to be deposited on shore with a record of our proceedings.

" In the meantime we had to keep steaming full speed to maintain our position against the wind, current, and ice. At 1 P.M., having seen our boat coming out through the ice, and again some distance off upon the ice-foot, with no one in it, a relief boat was manned ; but we soon saw our people rolling the cask of letters up the lower hill, about half a mile southward of the cape, when the recall was made, and by four o'clock they all returned on board, and Lieutenant Arbuthnot handed me a

copy of Captain Nares' record; the original, having blown from his hand
in a gust of wind, was lost in a valley of snow, the copy having, however,
been fortunately secured.

"I was too thankful to have our people safely on board after ten
hours' absence on such a stormy day, and on Lieutenant Arbuthnot
reporting that he had found nothing on the lower hill, excepting a
depôt of provisions, and there being every appearance of water to the
northward along the west land, we stood to the north-eastward under
steam and fore-and-aft canvas. I was glad to send below every one
who could be spared from the deck, most of us having been on duty
during the last thirty-six hours.

"At 9 P.M. we tacked and stood into Baird Inlet, but finding it full
of ice, we came out again, and continued northward until off Cape
Patterson, when the main pack was seen to extend close home upon the
land about Leconte Island, and on going to the crow's-nest I could see
that heavy streams were already coming down before the wind, and also
closing in from the eastward.

"Having in the meantime carefully considered Captain Nares' record,
and not feeling satisfied as to what Lieutenant Arbuthnot had actually
seen on Cape Isabella, and upon his assuring me that he had found four
cases and one cask, but no pemmican, I concluded that this could not
be a travelling depôt, that it was also too small for a retreating depôt,
and, moreover, from its being placed in the exact position in which
it was stated the despatches would be found, it was extremely probable that the cask seen contained those very despatches we were
looking for.

"I enclose Lieutenant Arbuthnot's own report of this visit to Cape
Isabella, which I trust will make this matter clearer to their Lordships.

"Our progress northward being stopped, I returned to Cape Isabella,
arriving there at 3 A.M. on the 7th of August. The ice had, however,
already come in, and the northerly gale again increasing, I was unable,
with full steam, to keep the ship sufficiently close without the risk of
her being forced upon the rocks.

"Under these circumstances, and expecting every moment to be beset
and carried off to the south-west or on shore, and considering the
extreme danger of detaching a party from the ship, I gave orders for
the boat to be secured, and stood off through the ice to the eastward.

"It is unnecessary to give the details of our proceedings in the
fortnight next following the 7th. I had decided to give up all idea
of trying Peel Straits this year, and to devote the remainder of the
navigable season to endeavouring to revisit Cape Isabella, and to pro-

ceed northward if necessary and possible, or at least to cruise the straits until the close of the season, in the event of a boat party or the Polar ships arriving, either of which, in the present aspect, seemed very doubtful.

" We continually crossed and recrossed the straits through the pack, always among ice, and keeping the ship constantly on the move to prevent our being beset. A boat and sledge were kept in readiness, and the officers repeatedly volunteered to attempt to reach the cape over the ice ; but although we forced the ship on several occasions within a few miles of the cape, the stormy weather, the sudden fogs, and rapid movements of the ice, all rendered it impossible to detach a party from the ship with any reasonable prospect of their reaching the cape or of rejoining the ship.

" The outer or eastern edge of the pack always presented one unbroken curve from the direction of Cape Dunsterville in the south-west round to Cairn Point, or Littleton Island, leaving a land water in Hartstene Bay.

" Into this water we always escaped when too hard pressed, and we were no less than three times, the 9th, 12th, and 22nd, driven into Pandora Harbour for a night's shelter.

" During the first week the winds remained from the northward, and large unbroken floes began to come down, one of which, on the 9th, appeared to fill the entire straits from side to side, and had six large icebergs imbedded in it. I had hopes that this would prove to be the first instalment after the breaking up of Kane's Basin, and that the straits might soon partially clear out.

" Once only, on the 15th, at the close of the north winds, the water made along the eastern shore as far as visible, and the hitherto persistent ice-sky in the north-west changed to a darker hue. I immediately pushed in, and thought that we might get round into water north of the pack ; but at midnight we came to the end of our lane in latitude 78° 45′ N., longitude 73° W., and there found the pack solid, and trending round upon the land near Cape Inglefield. It was a brilliantly clear and frosty night, with the temperature at 24° Fahrenheit, and we could see the land as far as Cape Scott on the east, and Cape Hawke on the west side. Several groups of walrus were lying on the ice, and we killed five of the largest size, yielding about four tons of flesh and oil.

" On the 19th, having driven back to the northward of Littleton Island, I visited Polaris Camp, in company with some of the officers. Nothing remained of the house beyond a few broken boards ; the rocks were strewn with pieces of metal and fragments of clothing, &c. I searched for the *cache* in which the instruments and books were placed by the retreating party, but I only found near its stated position a brass bowl of a 7-inch compass, a tin tube which might have contained the pendulum apparatus, and parts of a telescope. We found no cairn or any books of record.

"I collected a few relics, one being a lamp with 'S. Buddington' marked upon it; and, having left a record of our visit, we hastily embarked in our steam cutter, which carried us off through the heavy ice against a strong southerly wind. There were no signs of any recent visit of the Eskimos, but I noticed no less than five *caches* of walrus flesh, all in a putrid state.

"On the 23rd, the weather continuing very boisterous, and fearing that in entering the pack we were at any time liable to be surrounded and carried away into Baffin's Sea, I considered it the best for all concerned to place the despatches and remaining letters on Littleton Island. Consequently I landed with Lieutenant Arbuthnot at 10 P.M., and placed four cases and two casks in a cleft in the rocks, on the western point, where they would be invisible to the natives, and we left a notice in Captain Nares' cairn to that effect.

"The following morning, after a stormy night, we were among the drift ice, and observed that the main pack had slackened in the direction of Leconte Island. We immediately steamed into it, and were able, although the weather was thick, to keep moving in that direction until 8 P.M., when we were close over on the west land, the summit of the island showing up above the mist. At 10 P.M. the fog lifted, and we found ourselves in a large pool of land water, extending towards Cape Isabella. Going on full speed through some streams of drift and sheets of young ice, we arrived within a cable's length of the cape, on the morning of the 25th, just after midnight.

"The rocks were quite clear of ice, but some floes were streaming round the land from the southward before the wind and the current, which now ran to the north. The ship being placed close to the shore, Lieutenants Arbuthnot and Becker landed immediately, to visit the lower hill, taking tools, and bags to bring off the despatches, should the cask be found to contain them. They lost no time in ascending the hill, and returned safely on board after only an hour's absence. They reported that the cask was empty, and that the four cases contained preserved meat. It was now evident that no travelling or boat party had reached this position from the Polar ships, and that Captain Nares had deposited the cask on his outward journey as a receptacle for the despatches, in order to save its weight upon a sledge had a party been sent. A full record of our proceedings and a notice that letters had also been left on Littleton Island were placed magnetic north of this lower cairn.

" We had now spent the best period of the navigable season in our endeavours to regain this depôt, and in proportion as the difficulty of doing so had seemed to increase, so had the necessity appeared to arise for re-examining the cask, and the conviction that it had contained the despatches forced itself upon me, notwithstanding that I had fully weighed the improbability of any sledge party having been sent to the entrance of Smith Sound last spring, if the Expedition had succeeded in attaining the high latitude contemplated.

" Although all our efforts had thus resulted in not finding here any despatches of this year, we had at least deposited some letters at the appointed place, and I had the gratification of now feeling assured that the Polar ships had been so far successful as to reach such a distant position in the North as to render it inadvisable to send a sledge party to Cape Isabella for a merely secondary object.

" I again bore away to the northward under canvas. It was very dark and thick, but sufficiently clear to enable us to avoid the heavy ice. By 9 A.M. we were again up to Leconte Island, where we were stopped by a fog until eleven o'clock, when I could see from aloft that the main pack still extended across the straits into Rosse Bay. We were in a lake of land water, with close packed and heavy ice all round, from south to north, and again closing on the land from the eastward. Our only chance of moving seemed to be through a narrow lead or slack place, running first to the E.N.E., and then again apparently towards the east coast. We entered the pack, and succeeded by 5 P.M. in again escaping into the land water in Hartstene Bay.

" The navigable season was now fast drawing to a close, but it seemed too early to retire from the straits. I had decided to remain as late as possible, and as long as I could manœuvre the ship, although there was now no possibility of a boat party arriving, but I still had hoped that the Polar ships were on their way down, and that the ice might open and admit of their passing out. As, however, we could not move the ship in any direction excepting to the south, and being very fatigued, I ran for Pandora Harbour, which we found to be full of drift ice, and so we anchored in the bight outside.

" On the following morning, the 26th, the south-west pack was driving into Hartstene Bay, and threatening to shut us in ; so I weighed anchor and proceeded out, and we lay-to under the glacier by Cape Alexander all that day and night.

" On the 27th, still blowing hard from S.S.W., the ice continued to close and some floes had already entered our late anchorage, and lay across its entrance. We sailed out from under the glacier to the point of Cape Alexander, in order to obtain a better view, and found that a heavy pack had driven up from the south-westward upon the land south of the cape, off which there still remained about half a mile of water. To the southward and south-westward the sea was now covered with heavy ice and bergs, but we could still see open water about six miles due south from the cape. Our retreat thus appeared as if about to be cut off; and, as we could not remain in our present position, we had either to try to re-enter the harbour, there, probably, to be shut in for the winter, or to attempt to force out through the pack into the water seen in the south. There was no time to reflect, as a southerly storm was evidently approaching; so I chose the latter alternative, and immediately steamed into the slackest place in the pack, and succeeded by 2 P.M. in reaching the water, where we lay-to, with the engines going, during the following twenty-four hours, in a violent gale and snow storm. A breaking sea and the ice on each hand compelled us to tack the ship incessantly.

"August 28.—At 3 P.M. the gale moderated, and we saw that the ice had filled the straits and the head of Baffin's Bay right across and to about eight miles south of Cape Alexander. The pack extended in the S.W. as far as visible, but in the south there was open water, with a high swell rolling up from that direction.

" As we could not now re-enter the straits until some change should occur, and it was purposeless to remain outside in Baffin's Sea, I decided to proceed towards Upernivik, in North Greenland, upon the chance of finding that the last ship had not already sailed for Denmark, and in that case to send an officer home, and then return to Smith Straits. In arriving at this decision, I was guided by the conviction that either by remaining in our present position or in returning north we should very probably be overtaken by the frost, and have to remain during the winter, for which we were, however, fully prepared if necessary. We were all in good health, and our ship had received no serious damage beyond the bending of one of the blades of the propeller, which, however, considerably impeded our speed under steam.

" We therefore steered southward at 4 P.M., and on the following morning were off Hakluyt Island, having the pack always on our starboard hand until now, when it trended away in the direction of Clarence Head.

" As we had not met any of the natives, and being desirous of ascertaining where they were located in the event of our returning northward,

I steered for Bardin Bay, in Whale Sound. On entering the bay we soon observed a summer tent and some Eskimos, with their dogs, running to and fro, evidently to attract our attention. The bay was found to be full of reefs, and we had to back out and lay-to at the entrance. I then landed with several of the officers, taking with us Anthone, our Eskimo interpreter, in his kyak.

" The natives met us without fear, and helped to haul our boat on the shore. They consisted of the members of one family, ten in all, and appeared to have plenty of food; they were grateful, however, for some walrus flesh which I gave them. They were very communicative and natural in their manners. They told us that they had had a very good hunting season on account of the prevalence of much ice. They had seen no ships or white men for many years, but said that an old man, who lived with his family in Northumberland Island, saw two ships pass northward last summer. They had heard of the 'Polaris' wreck, but had not been so far north for some years, and I did not see anything in their possession to disprove their statement.

" I noticed among their treasures a ship's bucket, half the top of a mahogany table, a Greenlander's kyak paddle, much ice-worn, and a piece of packing-case marked 'Limejuice, Leith,' all of which they said had drifted into the bay at different times from the southward. This proves the existence of a permanent current to the northward along the coast from West Greenland and Melville Bay.

" These Eskimos, living in the extreme latitude of 77° 12' N., seemed to be a kind and simple people, robust and healthy. They offered us everything they had, and when asked what they would like to receive, the chief came off to the ship, and from all our treasures he selected a fifteen-foot ash oar and some gimlets. He wanted the oar for spear shafts, and the gimlets to bore ivory and bone in order to cut it. We gave them some other useful presents, and received some narwhal's horns, specimens of their pot-stone cooking kettles, and of the iron pyrites used for striking fire. We also exchanged some dogs, giving them five of ours for three of their finest bear-hunting and team dogs.

" Having taken leave of these interesting people, we sailed out of the bay in the evening, and continued our voyage towards Upernivik, where we arrived on the evening of September 7, after a stormy passage and much difficulty during the dark nights, with the quantities of icebergs on the coast. On the evening of the 6th we ran into the edge of the middle ice. It was, however, much broken into small floes, upon one of which I shot a remarkably fine Polar bear.

" The Governor of Upernivik came off to meet us, and informed me that the last ship had sailed on August 16, and he held out no hopes of our finding a ship for Europe at this late season in any of the more southern colonies.

" As we had now no opportunity of communicating with home, and considering that it would only complicate matters were we to be unavoidably detained the winter without the means of informing their Lordships, I anchored ship in the Danish harbour, and reluctantly gave orders to fill up with fresh water, and to refit for our return to England, according to our original intention, if nothing should occur to render it necessary for us to winter in the North.

" During our stay in Smith Sound we had taken every opportunity of sounding with Negretti's, or the Miller-Casella, thermometers attached, whenever practicable. The greatest depth was found in the middle of the straits, in the parallel of Cape Isabella, where it is 600 fathoms, and on this occasion a beautiful Asterias, measuring three feet in diameter, with the arms extended, was brought up from the bottom; it was quite alive, but very sluggish upon being landed on the deck.

" The ice we met in Smith Straits consisted of those solid pieces apparently formed near the shore in strong currents, and much pressed up by the action of the tides. These were intermingled with large and small floes, and much oceanic or Polar ice; the whole, from its deep draught of water, forming a pack of the heaviest description, and so unyielding as to render it unsafe to strike with any force, and consequently the more difficult to manœuvre a ship among it.

" With reference to the currents; after a month's constant cruising we arrived at the conclusion that there is a permanent current flowing northward on the east side, and southward on the west side, but not sufficiently strong to check the tides, the stream of the flood being always north, and of the ebb south, on both sides.

" We left Upernivik on the 11th, and arrived at Godhavn (Disco) on the night of the 15th, remaining there until the 21st, when I sailed for England, as I considered that if the ships were on their return home now they had already passed down Davis Straits.

" On our passage homeward we experienced calms, and light, variable winds during the first week, making but little progress; however, the weather soon changed, and set in with strong south-easterly and southerly gales, which continued almost without interruption until October 26, when we were 300 miles off the north-west of Ireland.

" We had, on the 1st of October, in Davis Straits, most unexpectedly met a quantity of heavy Spitzbergen drift ice in lat. 64° 31' N., long.

54° 40 W., and passed through a severe south-east gale among it the same night.

"On the 16th, in lat. 54° 38' N., long 44° 30' W., we sighted Her Majesty's ships 'Alert' and 'Discovery,' and bore away to communicate with them.

"We remained in company until the 19th, when we parted from the 'Discovery' in lat. 55° 39' N., long. 35° 48' W., and on the following day we experienced a hurricane from the south-west, with the barometer at 28·36.

"Complete series of magnetic observations were taken by Lieutenant Pirie, R.N., with both the 'Fox' and Jones' circles in North Greenland, and also in Pandora Harbour, in Smith Sound. The meteorological register was kept by Dr. Horner, and some interesting photographs were taken by Mr. W. Grant.

"In concluding this report, I have the honour of expressing to their Lordships how much I am indebted to Lieutenant C. R. Arbuthnot, R.N., and to Sub-Lieutenant G. Pirie, R.N., for their zealous and active services, and for the assistance they have rendered on all occasions; and I also avail myself of this opportunity of expressing the pleasure I have felt in having the honour of the association of two distinguished foreign officers, Lieutenant Alois Ritter von Becker, Austrian Imperial Navy, and Lieutenant Koolemans Beynen, Dutch Royal Navy, both of whom have shown the greatest zeal in the service on which we were engaged, and by their high attainments reflect infinite credit upon their noble profession. My ship's company also all conducted themselves to my entire satisfaction.

"I have the honour to forward herewith the two records of Captain Nares, from Littleton Island and Cape Isabella, also Captain Hartstene's, U.S.N., record from Sutherland Island, and the relics collected at the 'Polaris' camp, which, perhaps, might be acceptable to the United States Government."

LONDON : PRINTED BY WILLIAM CLOWES AND SONS, STAMFORD STREET AND CHARING CROSS.

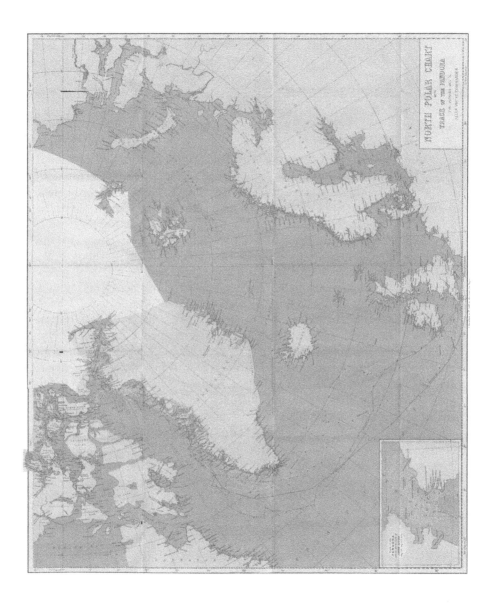

The material originally positioned here is too large for reproduction in this reissue. A PDF can be downloaded from the web address given on page iv of this book, by clicking on 'Resources Available'.